The punk explosion and beyond

Adrian Moulton was a special needs teacher for 40 years, teaching English, Drama and Music. A regular broadcaster on local radio, he still writes, records and performs with Reading's post-punk heroes The Complaints. Married, with children, step-children, grandchildren and great-grandchildren aplenty, he recently moved to Cornwall but finds he's still missing Reading. That'll wear off, surely?

Mike Warth was born and educated in Reading before completing teacher training at Milton Keynes College of Education. He taught in primary schools for 28 years, after which he was appointed as an Education Officer for Special Education, retiring in 2013. He is still working part-time in the Sound Machine in Reading and is the author of two books on local history, as well as a significant contributor to a series of books on rock music. Mike is married with children, stepchildren and grandchildren.

When Reading Really Rocked series

Volume 1: *The live music scene in Reading 1966–1976* by Adrian Moulton, Mike Warth and Austin Matthews
Volume 2: *The punk explosion and beyond* by Adrian Moulton with Mike Warth

Also published by Two Rivers Press

Reading Quaker Meeting: A history by Geoff Sawers & Izzy Brimelow
Downland: Paintings by Anna Dillon, Poems by Jonathan Davidson
Reading Poets: A new anthology edited by Vic Pickup
A Reading Scrapbook: A history of the town through printed ephemera by David Cliffe
Reading Gaol: A short history by Peter Stoneley
The Happy Prince by Oscar Wilde, hand lettered by Sally Castle
Coley Talking: Realities of life in old Reading by Margaret Ounsley
Bricks and Brickwork in Reading: Patterns and polychromy by Adam Sowan
Reading's Influential Women by Terry Dixon & Linda Saul
The Art and History of Whiteknights edited by Jenny Halstead
The Art of Peter Hay by John Froy with Martin Andrews
Signs of the Times: Reading's memorials by Malcolm Summers
Rural Reading by Adrian Lawson & Geoff Sawers
The Constitutionals: A work of fiction by Peter Robinson
Reading Abbey and the Abbey Quarter by Peter Durrant & John Painter
Reading's Bayeux Tapestry by Reading Museum
Picture Palace to Penny Plunge: Reading's cinemas by David Cliffe
Silchester: Life on the dig by Jenny Halstead & Michael Fulford
The Writing on the Wall by Peter Kruschwitz
Allen W. Seaby: Art and nature by Martin Andrews & Robert Gillmor
Fox Talbot and the Reading Establishment by Martin Andrews
All Change at Reading: The railway and the station, 1840–2013 by Adam Sowan
Cover Birds by Robert Gillmor
Caversham Court Gardens: A heritage guide by Friends of Caversham Court Gardens
Birds, Blocks and Stamps: Post & Go Birds of Britain by Robert Gillmor
Down by the River: The Thames and Kennet in Reading by Gillian Clark

When Reading Really Rocked,
volume 2:

The punk explosion and beyond

Adrian Moulton

with Mike Warth

First published in the UK in 2025 by Two Rivers Press
7 Denmark Road, Reading RG1 5PA
www.tworiverspress.com
info@tworiverspress.com

General Product Safety Regulations (GPSR) documentation:
www.tworiverspress.com/about/gpsr

© Two Rivers Press 2025
© in text Adrian Moulton with Mike Warth 2025

The right of the authors to be identified as the authors of this work has been asserted by them in accordance with the Copyright, Designs and Patents Act of 1988.

All rights reserved. No part of this publication may be reproduced, stored in or introduced into a retrieval system, or transmitted, in any form, or by any means (electronic, mechanical, photocopying, recording or otherwise) without the prior written permission of the publisher.

ISBN 978-1-915048-27-1

1 2 3 4 5 6 7 8 9

Two Rivers Press is represented in the UK by Inpress Ltd and distributed by BookSource, Glasgow.

Cover lettering and design by Sally Castle
Text design by Nadja Robinson and typeset in Parisine

Printed and bound in Great Britain by CMP (UK), Poole

Acknowledgements and picture credits

Special thanks to:

Mike Warth. A good friend and former colleague at The Sound Machine. A real hound dog of a researcher; if the information is out there, he'll track it down! His work, support and enthusiasm for this project ensured that it finally reached a happy conclusion.

Hannah Jackson. A former Reading University student and regular Sound Machine customer. She offered to go through the University's archive of *Shell* magazines at a time during the COVID-19 business when access to the archives was restricted to all but university staff. All information relating to musical activities at the university in this book has been possible through her dedication to the task. Thank you.

Neal Turner and Steve Edwards at The Sound Machine for offering me a job there when I retired from teaching and making all this possible. And to Chris Turner for patiently putting up with having to listen to endless Fall CDs when we worked together.

Thank you to the following for giving up their time to be interviewed for this project:

Iain Aird aka Sprog, Baz Barry, John Blaney, Mick Brock, Damian Clarke, Nick Duckett, Jez Dyer, Danny Fraifeld, Chris Green, Clive Hacker, Richard Jackman, Anne de Lima, Tony Long, Paul McColm, Denny Mills, Jo Morris, Greg Muden, Ian Mundwyler aka Mordecai Smyth, Noddy New, Colin Newton, Stewart Osbourne aka Eddie Snide, Neil Richards, Steve Rolfe, Billy Seago, Chris Trimby, Jimmy Yoder.

Thank you to the following for offering photographs, memorabilia and long-stored gems from the dusty recesses of their memory banks:

Terry and Nicola Allsop, Lars Bergen, James Carter, the late Mark Chapman, Alan Clayson, The Colour Mary, Hugh Crabtree, Brian Devoil, Mic Dover, Pete Downs, Chris Green, Steve and Jacqui Gresswell, Tim Hill, Tim Hulse, Matt Hulse, Shaun Philip Hutchings, Peter Judd, Andrew King, Mark Lauri, Rob Lewis, Richard Linton, Tony Long,

Darrell Mitchell, Jonathan Mitchell, Sandy Monteith, Graham Morris, Owen Mott, Paul Murphy, Colin Newton, Chewy Newton, Philip Nixon, Barry O'Brien aka The Fence, Alan 'Oggi' Orgill, Ian Parsons, Steve Rolfe, Alison Rolls, Andy Rowe, Peter Rowe, Rainer Schmidt, James Sedge, Richard Seymour, Dave Soper, Lou Spyrou, Kenny Stone, Soo Toombs, John Townsend, Simon Wright, Trevor Young.

And the staff at the following libraries:

Reading Central Library, The British Library, London and University of Reading Library ... at least they let Hannah in!

Also very special thanks to Anne Nolan and Nadja Robinson, and all at Two Rivers Press.

Picure credits

While every effort has been made to trace the copyright holders and obtain permission to reproduce the photographs included in this book, we would like to apologise should there have been any errors or omissions. Please do get in touch with any enquiries or any information relating to images which we have been unable to credit.

x: © *Sideburns;* 5 (band photo): Ian Dickson/Shutterstock; 5 (ticket): Pete Downs; 9: Adrian Moulton; 11: Public domain; 14–16: Richard Linton; 19: Fair use; 22: © Terry Allsop; 24: Fair use; 25: Richard Linton; 27: Courtesy of Stephen Rolfe; 29: Courtesy of Stephen Rolfe; 30: Graham Racher CC BY-SA 2.0 (https://en.wikipedia.org/wiki/Danielle_Dax#/media/File:Danielle_Dax.jpg); 33: Fair use; 35: Courtesy of Alison Rolls; 37: © *Grinding Halt;* 38: unknown photographer; 41: unknown photographer; 42: Fair use; 45: Public domain; 46: Courtesy of Rainer Schmidt; 47: Courtesy of Rainer Schmidt; 49: Courtesy of Jez Dyer; 50: Public domain; 51: Peter Rowe; 52: Graham Morris; 53: Barbara Mundwyler; 56: © *Grinding Halt;* 59 (The Complaints): unknown photographer; 59 (Johnny Thunders): Thomas Good CC BY-SA 4.0 (https://en.wikipedia.org/wiki/Johnny_Thunders#/media/File:NLN_Johnny_Thunders.jpg); 60: Courtesy of Tony Long; 65: Matthew Mawford; 67 (Patti Smith): UCLA Library

Special Collections CC BY-SA 2.0 (https://commons.m.wikimedia.org/wiki/File:Patti_Smith,_1978_%28cropped%29.jpg); 67 (Pauline Murray): Jos van Vliet CC BY-SA 4.0 (https://en.wikipedia.org/wiki/Pauline_Murray); 67 (Siouxsie Sioux): Malco23 CC BY-SA 3.0 (https://commons.wikimedia.org/wiki/File:Siouxsie_sioux.jpg); 67 (Tina Weymouth): Michael Markos CC BY-SA 2.0 (https://commons.m.wikimedia.org/wiki/File:Tina_Weymouth,_1977.jpg); 68: Courtesy of Paul McColm; 70: unknown photographer; 71: unknown photographer; 73: Courtesy of Mic Dover; 74: Mic Dover CC BY-SA 4.0 (https://commons.wikimedia.org/wiki/File:Friciton_Groove_live_gig.jpg); 76 (Geisha Girls): Fair use; 76 (The Complaints): Fair use; 79: Courtesy of Adrian Moulton; 80: Courtesy of Rainer Schmidt; 83: Courtesy of Adrian Moulton; 85: © *Kiss This*; 86: © *Grinding Halt*; 88 (*Exposure* fanzine): © *Exposure*; 88 (*Utterance* fanzine): © *Utterance*; 90: Fair use; 93: Courtesy of Stephen Rolfe; 94: © Steve Gresswell; 96: Fair use; 101: © *Grinding Halt*; 105: © David Payne; 107: © Peter Rowe; 110: Fair use; 112: Fair use; 114 (The Target): Courtesy of Paul Murphy; 114 (Reading Trades Union): © Terry Allsop; 115: Courtesy of Rainer Schmidt; 116: © Terry Allsop; 119: Courtesy of Stephen Rolfe; 122: Courtesy of Clive Hacker; 125: Courtesy of Stephen Rolfe; 127: Courtesy of Alan Orgill; 129: Courtesy of Rainer Schmidt; 130: Courtesy of Lars Bergen; 131: Andrew King CC BY-SA 2.0 (https://upload.wikimedia.org/wikipedia/commons/7/78/Whitesnake-1980.jpg); 132: Courtesy of Lars Bergen; 133: © James Sedge; 134: © Shaun Philip Hutchings; 136: Fair use; 138: © Gary Harman, courtesy of The Colour Mary; 139: Greg Neate CC BY-SA 2.0 (https://commons.wikimedia.org/wiki/File:Slowdive_live_1992.jpg); 141: Chris Broderick; 142: Adrian Moulton; 143: Courtesy of Andy Rowe; 144: Courtesy of Peter Rowe; 145: Courtesy of Rainer Schmidt; 146: © *Sideburns*; 149: Courtesy of Lou Spyrou

Enjoy our
**When Reading
Really Rocked, volume 2**
YouTube playlist

Contents

What Makes for a Local Scene? | 1

Introduction | 2

  1. Something Better Change | 4
  2. We Few. We Seething Few | 13
  3. The Good Times are Just Around the Corner | 32
  4. Punk Goes to College, Reluctantly | 40
  5. Let's Put the Show on Right Here! | 51
  6. The Bulmershe Connection | 62
  7. Working For You | 81
  8. A Dummy's Guide to Setting Up Your Own Record Label | 89
  9. Appearing in Town Tonite! | 100
10. Pick up the Pieces | 113
11. Never Trust the Weather | 121
12. And Here Come the 90s | 135

Stand Up and Be Counted:
Reading Bands 1977–1987 | 140

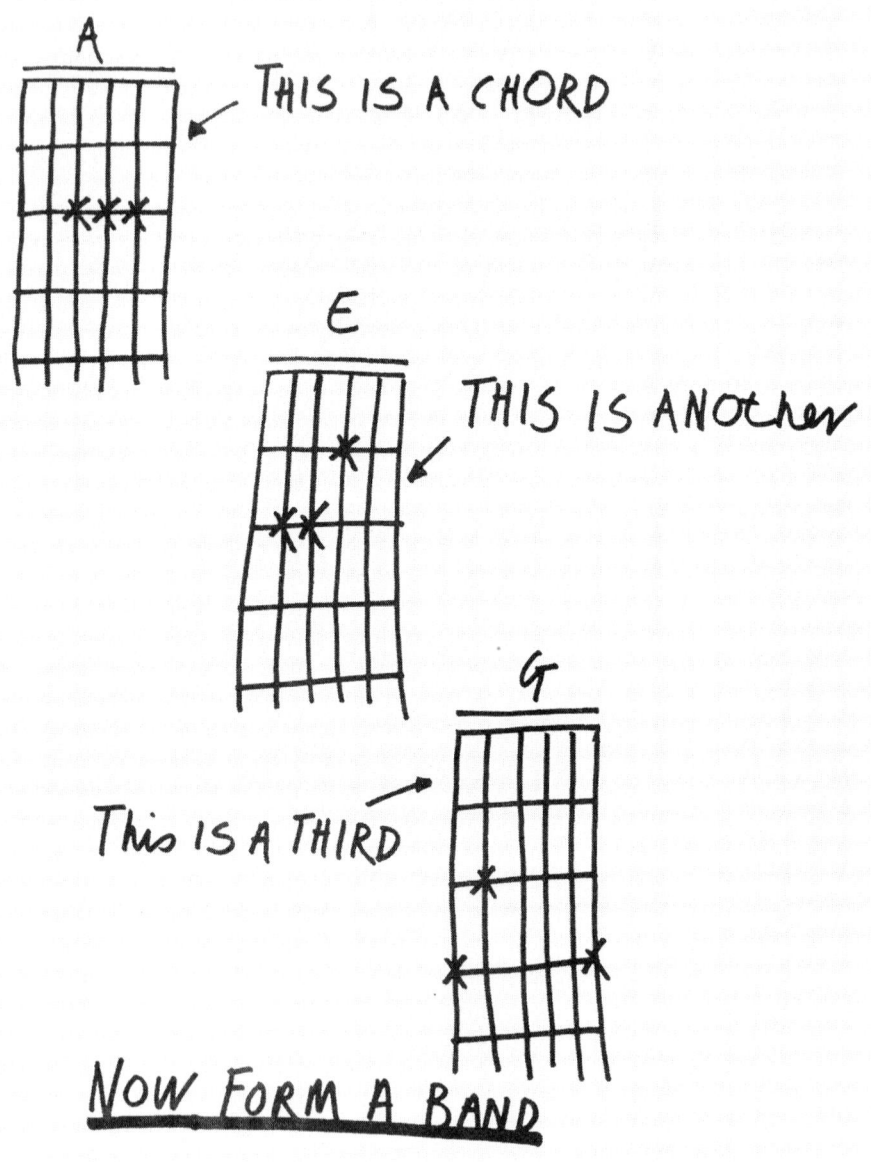

What Makes for a Local Scene?

Many people I spoke to for this book felt they were a part of a vibrant local music scene in the late 70s and 80s. So what actually serves to make a local scene happen? Darrell Mitchell of Home And Abroad suggested that you needed the following to be in place:

- a number of sympathetic venues that were happy to regularly promote locally-based singers and bands;
- a sizeable number of people who wanted to listen to locally-based singers and bands playing mostly original material;
- a DJ to champion it all on the radio;
- small labels to help the singers and bands release their material.

I would add one more to the list:

- lively, independent fanzines to document and discuss all that was happening. There was, of course, no internet and no social media.

This was all in place in Reading back in the late 70s and 80s. And as Darrell says today:

"We were lucky to be a part of this moment in time."

Indeed we were.

Opposite page: A musical call to arms from an early fanzine, *Sideburns*, from January 1977

Introduction

Paul McColm's father had played the trumpet in The Amboy Dukes, arguably Reading's top band during the 1960s, and after spending most of the 1970s in Australia, the family returned to their hometown, with young Paul eager to follow in his father's musical footsteps. But things back home had changed somewhat. Let him take up the story:

> "I stepped out into the cultural maelstrom that was punk. Coming back to the UK was like stepping into a mash-up of *Quadrophenia* and *A Clockwork Orange*. Everywhere you looked there were different tribes; skinheads, teds, rockers, punks, dreads, it was a real culture shock. But it was the best place to be for the music, which was astonishing. I wanted to be part of that."

This book is a continuation of the story of some of the major activities that took place in the musical life of the town of Reading, this second volume centring on the emergence of punk in the late 70s and its continued influence on the multitude of ever-changing styles that emerged in the 80s. It's about how the do-it-yourself ethic inherent within the punk movement inspired a new generation to continually update their musical vision, the energy and imagination unleashed reinvigorating the musical life of the town. Many of those involved are still wreathed in smiles to this day as they recollect the escapades and excitement of the times, those precious years when their teenage identities were being forged in the white heat of punk's fiery furnace.

On 1 December 1976 I was deep into the final year of my degree course at Bulmershe College, the world outside passing me by virtually unnoticed. I'd heard of punk. I'd even heard of The Sex Pistols but it all seemed to be happening somewhere else. I remember a fellow student announcing in a tutorial that her brother had become a roadie for some band called The Clash. None of us had heard of them. But by the early evening of Wednesday 1 December 1976, the whole country knew a whole lot more about the subject, a direct result of the early evening screening of a confrontation between a much-respected journalist and TV presenter, Bill Grundy, and his guests, The Sex Pistols, which followed on from a video of the band performing their debut single, 'Anarchy In The U.K.'.

It was here that Joe Public came face to face with punk rockers, busy revelling in their full-on, spittle-flecked defiance of convention, Johnny Rotten's sneering, snot-drenched aural assault centre-stage. Anarchy? Anti-Christ? A desire to destroy passers-by? Wow! This was not your standard tea-time fare. No trigger warnings in those days. The national press had a field day as parody and fear stalked the land.

Within a couple of weeks, the end of term celebrations at Bulmershe included a student band, their ripped clothing held together by safety pins, pretending to be sick into a bucket! Oh, how we laughed! And driving through central London a few days later I spied a group of the genuine article looking somewhat conspicuous among the be-denimed masses. "I wanna see punks!" cried my daughter Coralie from the back seat. Although punk had been around for almost a year, up to the beginning of December 1976 future Reading-based record boss Chris Green could claim that "punk had been the best kept secret in the land". Obviously not anymore if even my four-year-old could be so obviously enthused.

I lived and worked in the town all through these turbulent, tumultuous musical times, attending as many gigs as I could, first as a fan and then, like so many others desperate to become involved, I joined a group. It was, for the most part, an awful lot of fun. I hope that comes across in the following pages.

For further reading, may I recommend to you Chris Green's *Criminal Damage And Other Misadventures*, for his peerless insights into being both a Reading punk and the creator and driving force behind the Criminal Damage record label.

Adrian Moulton
December 2024

1. Something Better Change

The First Stirrings

It had been six months since the Bill Grundy interview on Thames Television's Today programme, where viewers came face to face with what most regarded as the stuff of pop nightmares. It had taken a while, but on a Monday night on 13 June 1977 the recently spawned punk disciples of Reading, nurtured in the sympathetic surroundings of pubs like The Star, finally got their chance to gather unto one another and celebrate, for The Jam, and their support act The Boys, were appearing that night amid the Come Dancing sequinned splendour of The Top Rank Ballroom, conveniently sited over the Reading bus depot.

The handful that had been hip to the new beat for some time were perhaps entitled to feel slightly superior mingling with all these late comers. Theale Green pupil Chris Green was one of those who'd long been in the know:

> "it felt very much like a fifth-form, fancy dress disco. Hugely embarrassing".

But artistic movements of any significance attract new disciples or die, people like Jimmy Yoder for instance, for whom this was the start of a lifetime's love affair with the genre:

> "from this moment I started to wear safety pins and badges and colour my hair with a felt tip pen".

Up first that night were The Boys, a true punk band in sound, attitude and looks, coming across as seriously pissed off but managing to express their discontent with a welcome dash of humour. They offered the perfect start to the night, according to Meadway pupil Mick Brock, delighting in the opportunity to sport a ripped jacket held together with safety pins amongst the comparative safety of a like-minded crowd. Being a punk was, after all, a lifestyle choice that came with trouble attached.

Opposite page: The Jam at Top Rank Reading, 13 June 1977

The Jam delivered that mathematical impossibility, one hundred and ten per cent, in terms of energy and commitment, and doing considerably more than just tipping their hats to the previous generation's thrusting, pill-popping mod trailblazers, The Who and The Small Faces. Now here were The Jam, their ultra mod styling a throwback to the mid-60s, right at home within this punk vortex. With a Who-style Union Jack draped across their retro Vox amplification, their snappy suits, smart shoes and haircuts, they somehow fitted right in. And the songs were catchy, politically charged, full of hooks and lyrically intelligent, their delivery like a force of nature.

Reading Evening Post's on-the-spot correspondent noted both the band's undoubted energy and the fact that they were called back for two encores, but seemed unhappy that this cavernous dance palace looked half empty:

> "Alright, where were you? Once again Reading has earned
> its reputation as a town of stay-at-home people".

Really? Five hundred and fifty people is not a bad turn out on a Monday night for a band whose first recording had only recently scraped into the Top 40, and it's quite possible that many young punks may have felt that a venue like The Rank just wasn't a natural hangout for a movement centred on notions of anarchy. Besides, £1 admission, or £1.20 on the door may sound like a puny amount today but it was far from being so in 1977. A couple of months previously I remember finding a fifty pence piece in the gutter and feeling like I'd won the pools!

By all accounts, and on all levels, the evening was a great success for a movement only just beginning to emerge from the shadowlands of the pubs and clubs of the Big City. Late to join the party, perhaps, but this mostly Reading-based legion of young punks had at last been given the opportunity to usher in this new musical age together.

Prior to this, for the first six months of 1977, the opportunities for punks to celebrate punk style and music were few in the Borough. Chris Green already knew the score, having attended the 100 Club Punk Festival back in September 1976 where he witnessed first-hand a performance by The Sex Pistols. It was life changing:

> "I had never seen anything like it ... [and] from that very first
> second I instinctively knew that I could do whatever I wanted to
> do and be whatever I wanted to be".

If you were one of those who had caught on to the fact that the musical times were indeed changing back in 1976 and you lived within the Reading area, you were going to have to travel. However, this didn't necessarily mean a trip to the Smoke. Ron Watts may have become famous as the promoter of punk's breakout gigs at the 100 Club but his regular gig was in a tiny upstairs room at The Nag's Head in High Wycombe and had been since the late 60s. Through the latter part of 1976 punk bands, The Pistols included, featured in the club's listings. On 18 November The Clash made one of their early appearances, supported by Reading's already well established art-school rockers Clayson and The Argonauts. Backstage, Alan Clayson found this thrusting young outfit quite hard work to share a cramped dressing room with as they seemed determined to live up to punk's rapidly coalescing image of being faintly aggressive, stand-offish, condescending and aloof. This was not a gig Clayson remembers too fondly. Argonaut guitarist Mic Dover described his evening as being

> "a white riot glimpse of the future, instantly making you feel you were part of the past; a realisation that your medium-length hair and flares should immediately be consigned to the cultural dustbin, along with ninety per cent of the guitar chords you thought you needed to learn."

Simplicity was the name of the game now. Nobody was looking to make a career out of punk. Well, not at the start anyway. The point was that the music could be quite basic, and the level of musical competence needed to join the party could be gained within a matter of weeks, not years. But it was the attitude that was the important thing. Cut out the guitar solos and keep your material short and intense. In other words, climb onto that stage, make your point, leave.

Now, XTC were anything but basic musicians, but they had the looks, the attitude and the material. And they were among the first true punk bands to appear in the town, turning up in early February at The Target, the long-established live music bar below the Butts Centre. Those Swindon boys played there three times in the early months of the new year and the place was hot, sweaty, smoky and packed each time. Local art teacher Clive Hacker, soon-to-be leader of his own mischievous band of art-punks, The Great Mistakes, was most impressed by them:

"They were technically very proficient, but punk through and through. Singer Andy Partridge was totally manic and frighteningly intense, and this fitted the scene perfectly".

The music was spiky and jerky, abruptly stopping and starting, torn, tight and intense, surrounding the highly mannered, strung-out-sounding voice of Andy Partridge. Add a 60s garage-sounding organ and some scratchy, shaky guitar and it all sounded kinda n-n-nervous, especially with all the low frequencies removed, the better to enhance the experience of those listeners zonked out on the punk's drug of choice, speed. Apparently.

Disciples were going to have to travel if they wanted a regular taste of the new action however, and their most likely destination other than High Wycombe was, of course, London, the planet Jupiter to little 'ol Reading's Callisto. But then, in early March, Bulmershe College took a punt promoting those cartoon funsters The Vibrators. Not destined to be one of the greats, perhaps, but a proper punk band, and for many in the less-than-packed Bridges Hall that night a first encounter with the real thing. The band exuded the studied dumbness of those true pioneers The Ramones and operated at about the same tempo, but there was less of The Shangri-La's about them and a bit more of the Glitter Band. Wearing combinations of leopard-print strides, PVC jackets and 50s-style shades they played nothing over a minute and a half and were surprisingly competent, their sneeriness a bonus.

Many of those present had turned up out of curiosity and, inevitably, there was some hostility. Plastic beer mugs, some half full, were lobbed in the band's direction quickly bringing the night's entertainment to a close. Obviously expecting this, the quartet downed tools, called us all a bunch of student wankers and left the stage to a smattering of applause drowned out by a cacophony of abuse. We'd got twenty minutes of punk rock for our money.

I bought the whole punk package that night and couldn't stop smiling. And I wasn't the only one.

Knox of The Vibrators on stage at Bulmershe, March 1977

Do Something Muttley!

Somehow punk had to happen. Inflation in the UK was in double figures for the fourth year in a row. Industrial disputes dominated the headlines and the country seemed set on establishing the reputation for grimness at the tail-end of the decade that is familiar even to those lucky enough to be too young to remember. Although Reading was fortunate to escape the worst of it, scapegoats for the nation's economic woes were identified and targeted by the terminally stupid and proudly racist National Front, revelling in the violence that inevitably accompanied their provocative determination to march through areas of towns characterised by high unemployment and rising levels of immigration.

This was a time when only a tiny percentage of school leavers went on to university, very few of whom were from a working class or ethnic minority background. For everybody else the prospect of the dole, or at best a dead-end job, loomed large. Step forward The Sex Pistols.

Their music was hardly revolutionary but the singer, and the singer's lyrics, were something else altogether. Not since the late 60s and Detroit's MC5 had a rock band been this confrontational or sound this dangerous and it was all thanks to Johnny Rotten's demonic-sounding disenchantment and his abrasive, confrontational lyrics, murdering any lingering semblance of deference in the year the Queen celebrated her Silver Jubilee.

It was a direct response to a crap education system, shoddy housing and the prospect of unemployment. No future indeed, and all on a Labour government's watch, fuelling the sense that there was nowhere else to turn. Snotty, sweary kids they might be, but their musical stance posted teenage rebellion as full-on political activism. Fighting-mad and armed with a voice that transformed anger into an aural threat, Johnny Rotten made the prospect of anarchy in the UK seem a likely and very worrying prospect, hence the huge levels of public antagonism levelled against anyone brave enough to stick their punky young heads above the parapet, something a Reading lad like Mick Brock was patently aware of. After all, post-Grundy, everybody in Britain now held an opinion on punk, be it amused condescension or outright hostility. Chris Green describes life as a young punk in Reading during those early months, not only avoiding

The Sex Pistols in 1977, the same line-up that played Reading University Fine Art Dept in May 1976, and before Glen Matlock was replaced by Sid Vicious.

confrontations with groups of Teds and Skinheads but everybody else as well:

> "...we were treated like alien invaders, fearful shoppers grabbing hold of their kids and parting like the Red Sea as we passed through."

Oratory School pupil Stewart Osborne was instantly inspired by the snarling face of punk and identified with it immediately. Rather small for his age and seen as a bit of an outsider, he felt his fellow pupils hated him:

> "And I hated them. And then punk came along. Punks were getting attacked in the streets and I thought, welcome to my world!"

Faced with a grim, uncertain future punk arrived to offer the anxious, angry youth of the nation an opportunity to join the party. Don't like what's going on in Britain? Then make yourself heard! Have fun! Create chaos!

And there was this musical call to arms from an early fanzine, *Sideburns*, from January 1977:

"This is a chord. This is another. This is a third. Now form a band."

It was as if punks were personally inspired by those immortal words of Dick Dastardly to his dog, invariably uttered in moments of panic and alarm:

"Don't just sit there! Do something Muttley!"

And they did. They formed bands, started fanzines and record labels. They became promoters and opened record shops. They set up studios and rehearsal spaces, became sound engineers and radio presenters, all in an environment where sexual orientation wasn't an issue. Demo tapes, flexi discs and self-financed record releases proliferated and were played by sympathetic DJs, nationally by the movement's most influential supporter, John Peel. Punk gigs were not like other musical entertainments; they were exciting, energy-stuffed physical affairs where the pogo was the only dance possible in the jam-packed sweaty confines of clubs like Bones. Jimmy "the punk" Yoder became a bone fide local hero dancing in his own inimitable style in such surroundings, although his one and only visit to that legendary venue saw him ejected after five minutes for being under-age!

Ah, yes! The Jubilee. It was ironic that the Queen had to celebrate her Silver Jubilee when the nation was in such a financial and cultural pickle. Street parties and bunting proliferated whilst we pop pickers propelled The Sex Pistols' 'God Save The Queen' to the top of the charts. I bought the record. I also attended a rather good street party. Never turn down a free tea!

And whilst all this was going on, across the nation, and across our town, a new generation was staying up way past its bedtime, working on those three chords and getting ready to join the fray. Let's meet some of them.

2. We Few. We Seething Few

Mister Nick Duckett

In the months following Bill Grundy's career-ending encounter with punk, bands began to spring up across the valley like the sown teeth of the Hydra. From Bracknell came The Infra-Red Helicopters and from Crowthorne, those merry pranksters The K9s. Trash were from Weybridge but had relocated to Zinzan Street "in order to cash in on the new cultural centre of Britain." Or so they told local fanzine Kiss This. The Romantix and General Accident were Reading boys through and through. Mostly.

The Borough already had a thriving music scene, of course, but these new combos gleefully set about spooking the horses. No, the world was not turned upside down overnight, but it was rattled, as these upstarts began to muscle their way into the picture. Bands still wrote prog epics and headbanging anthems, and soul, reggae, disco and funk outfits still sold out The Top Rank, whilst most bookings for The Target remained standard, if often excellent, rock fare.

Punk fans were a boisterous lot, a reputation well established by the middle of 1977, and they also tended to attract violent opposition from those less enamoured of the style, which made promoters anxious and less likely to book them. They needed a saviour, preferably one of their own. Step forward Mr Nick Duckett.

Nick had arrived from Manchester to read German at the University, choosing Reading because he rather liked the idea of studying where the annual rock festival was staged. Graduating in the summer of 1977 he, with university research officer Richard Linton and three or four others, set themselves up in a house in the upmarket enclave of St Peter's Avenue in Caversham Heights, their prospective landlord arriving for the viewing in a gold Rolls Royce, unaware that these young men had every intention of turning the house into the wildest place going. They succeeded simply and spectacularly by throwing a party at which two bands happened to be playing. With Nick's own crew The Beevers playing in his bedroom, those boys from Zinzan Street, Trash, were invited to play in the garage. Perhaps surprisingly, all went well. Nick wrote a review of the event and somewhat tongue-in-cheek sold it to the press as a bold and spectacular opening

The audience at The Garage on opening night, 25 January 1978

night of a new punk venue, The Garage. The national music press took the bait and published his account word for word. But with attendance reported at around the hundred mark all these punks had been wandering around Caversham wondering where on earth this "Garage" place was, and there were bound to be repercussions. One evening a few days later Richard came across a man with some sound equipment and a clipboard creeping around outside the house, so, unsurprisingly perhaps, the neighbours must have complained.

Attempts were made to have Nick and his fellow occupants evicted, but an ineptly constructed case against them was thrown out of court, and over the next year he managed to stage three further events of a similar magnitude before his landlord, having obviously been leant on by the neighbours, offered him a sum of money to vacate, which he did. Richard was long gone, but Nick departed leaving behind

Nick Duckett in his Caversham bedroom in 1978

some assorted punks squatting in the spare rooms upstairs. Let 'em sort that one out, were his departing thoughts.

Richard and Nick became good friends, with the former marvelling at the extent of Nick's various musical activities. These included second-hand record dealing, placing ads in the local press to secure the raw material needed to trade with, band management with a bunch of lads from Swindon going out under the name of Urban Disturbance, and, of course, promotions. Musical minimalist punk innovators Wire were booked for The Nag's Head in High Wycombe, a gig that descended into chaos. Nick was adamant that the trouble had been caused by agent provocateurs, after all this was legendary promoter Ron Watts' home turf and the Big Man had already physically warned Nick off, throwing him against a wall. It worked.

Soon-to-be punk superstars Siouxsie and The Banshees on stage in Bones Club, April 1978

He was also in at the start with Bones Club, the lease having been bought by two ex-boxers who needed some advice on the direction they needed to take. Having already established his credentials with the town's budding punk scene he was asked to DJ at the newly monikered establishment and decided to bring in his chum Mike Read. Yes, that's the Mike Read of radio and TV fame. At the time Mike was with Radio 210 and was, somewhat surprisingly, eager to become involved. Nick had got to know him by phoning up his show and teasing him on-air, but the two of them established a rapport nonetheless. Nick describes Mike as being a lovely bloke but very, very showbizzy, a trait that would seem to have been somewhat at odds with his professed love of the New Wave.

Running for just over a year, the aptly-named Bones occupied a former mortuary round the back of what was still Heelas, having been converted into a club in the mid-60s and undergone multiple makeovers subsequently. One memorable night featured those new punk superstars Siouxsie and The Banshees, their set being recorded for posterity by The Rolling Stones' mobile studio whose equipment inconveniently filled up half the club. Richard Linton was there with his camera, snapping away from the side of the stage and capturing images of that fabulous night. Tubeway Army played there, with Gary Numan at their head and, reputedly, Generation X with Billy Idol, although they were advertised and cancelled so many times no one seems able to confirm whether they actually ever set foot in the place. Slaughter and the Dogs most certainly did, as did Swindon's future multiple hit-makers XTC. Then there were The Damned, who appeared under the pseudonym The Doomed due to some contractual shenanigans. Future Great Mistakes' front man Clive Hacker danced on stage with female punk pioneers The Slits until he was unceremoniously booted back into the crowd to much applause. And Steve Rolfe's first visit to the club was life-changing:

> "I remember walking down the stairs and the heat hit you first. The K9s were onstage doing a cover of The Damned's 'New Rose'. I walked into this atmosphere of heat and sweat with everyone jumping about like crazy and I was like...Wow!"

And it is the K9s, along with those other local superstars General Accident, whose appearances in the club are most fondly recalled. Jimmy The Punk may have failed to gain entry to the premises, but he turned up regularly nonetheless, listening to the likes of Pauline Murray and Penetration from the shadows of St Mary's churchyard across the road, dancing the night away.

The place probably held a couple of hundred souls at a push, but Nick remembers that it was often far from full. You queued up on the outside, went up some steps to get in and then descended another twenty down into the smoky, sweltering heart of the beast. It was a short-lived enterprise, surviving for little more than a year, but managed to pack into that time appearances by some of the legends of the new wave, hosted a series of all-day festivals and provided the town's punks with life-long memories of somewhere very special.

Nod, Tramp and General Accident

There was an aura of menace and authenticity that hung over General Accident, an aura which distinguished and separated them from their contemporaries and which they shared with the likes of the national brand leaders, The Sex Pistols and The Clash. That made them special. And this was Noddy and Tramp's band, two likely lads who had been friends since they were kids sharing a love of motorbikes and The Rolling Stones. Nod took up the drums, Tramp tried his hand at the bass.

The pair worked for a local employment agency, smoking copious amounts of dope to alleviate the tedious nature of the tasks on offer and placing bets with each other to see how quickly they could get the sack. A position in a mattress factory lasted under an hour and included a nap lying flat out on the stock. If punk was going to enthuse anyone it was these two.

Pete Cox, a talented musician, arranger and friend who later worked so successfully with Alan Clayson, liked Tramp's Mick Jagger impression and, recognising his potential, recruited him just in time for his own band to audition for a West End production of a play called *The Soldiers Are Coming*, the story being told through the lyrics of the songs. They got the job, their success down to Tramp's obvious on-stage charisma. For an eighteen-year-old lad from Calcot this was quite a break.

Right on cue, punk arrived. As Nod says today:

> "you didn't have to be a good musician. Punk brought it all down to street level. Ordinary working-class kids could get themselves into a band."

Teaming up with John Copplestone on guitar and Chris Broderick on bass, General Accident were born, late 1977. Here at last was a local outfit with punk's required drive and attitude and at their first appearance in Woodley they were mobbed by punk-starved kids eager to learn where the next one was. It was at Bones Club,

The cover of the General Accident release, Look Alright/Trouble Makers that was recorded in 1977

of course, supporting The Lurkers, a band with whom they were musically well matched.

Momentum gathered pace, and support slots turned into headline appearances, the doors having to be locked against the overwhelming crowds turning up to see them at The Target. The Star pub on Duke Street became the meeting place for their fans to gather and as many as three coaches had to be hired to take followers to out of town appearances. Coming third in a Battle of the Bands contest at The Hexagon prompted their disgruntled fans to cause mayhem, and much grief for General Manager Tim Hulse as he strove to restore order, with further trouble seemingly just around the corner since the boys had been sharing the stage with a genuine General Accident sign stolen from the global insurance company's Newbury office. The local papers had a field day, but for a punk band this was manna from heaven. A short time later Tramp was arrested for fly posting, and as the new bad boys on the local scene the papers reported that too. But as Nod says:

> "All this publicity was brilliant. We weren't murderers, just a band that stuck two fingers up at the bollocks we all had to put up with."

Not looking to get rich or famous, they loved playing live and, like a street gang, watched each other's backs. This was crucial to both their success and their appeal, their live appearances becoming increasingly intense affairs. An Abingdon School show turned into a full-blown riot as fans went on the rampage when somebody pulled the plug on their fearsomely passionate performance. Mick Brock remembers the chaos of these gigs away from Reading:

> "You'd get the local youths after you and it could all get a bit hectic. They were often rough affairs. There were always punch-ups."

Two young lads present that night in Abingdon were nonetheless inspired enough to go and form their own gang, eventually settling on the name Radiohead.

Healthy music scenes mutate surprisingly quickly, and the Coventry-based 2 Tone re-imagining of ska alongside the increasing popularity and influence of reggae was picked up by the more forward-looking outfits who now gave their working-class angst a hybrid punk/reggae feel by simply using upstrokes on the guitar and adding a whole lot of echo to proceedings and at the same time managing to remain both relevant and authentic. General Accident took this route and created the perfect musical backdrop for Tramp's Jagger/Geldof nasal intonation and Nod's precise, undemonstrative drumming.

In November 1980 their big break finally arrived when they appeared alongside The Specials on the BBC early evening youth programme *Something Else* and more than held their own. They contributed two reggae-inflected numbers called 'Walking On The Right Side' and the maddeningly catchy 'Elephants in Stilettos', their performance in front of a live studio audience sparkling with both wit and charisma.

Post transmission Nod's phone rang hot with record labels eager to sign them up, including those big beasts EMI and Virgin. Unfortunately for all concerned this was the exact moment that Tramp's past came back to haunt him. Big time. The show went out on Tuesday. By Friday he was starting a two-and-a-half-year prison sentence.

Nod and Tramp had been on the police radar for years as keen smokers of weed and their Purley house had already been raided when, for reasons far too complex to relate here, they were suspected of importing industrial amounts of the stuff from India. Although the police found virtually nothing in the house it was obvious this wasn't going to be the end of the matter. Tramp foolishly agreed to sell some amphetamine sulphate for two rogue chemists who were manufacturing industrial amounts of the stuff while working at Gillette's on the Basingstoke Road. The story filled the local press when the arrests of all those concerned were announced, with the police firmly believing that the whole band had to be involved in distributing the drugs somehow. This was not so, but it was effectively the end for GA who limped on briefly playing benefit shows to raise cash to send Tramp some goodies while inside.

Nod has this to say about the band's musical adventures in the liner notes for a recent General Accident compilation:

> "We were the right age, we had the right look, the right songs, the right attitude... and we were in the right place at the right time."

Exactly. Nobody deserved the breaks more than they did, and they came tantalisingly close to breaking through. It should be some compensation to know that no band from the Reading area is more fondly remembered, their on-stage mannequin dressed as a copper adding a dash of defiance and bravado to their legend.

The Star

This pub, just across the hump-back bridge over the Kennet, and central to the punk experience in the town during the late 70s, is long gone. It was bulldozed some years later when the whole area was being revamped, the enormous Courage brewery making way for The Oracle and the completion of the optimistically named Inner Distribution Road. It had long had something of a reputation, both for good and for slightly dodgy reasons.

A typical town centre pub, a bit scruffy perhaps and certainly nothing special architecturally, I first visited with my girlfriend Jennie at the tail-end of 1970, she informing me that it was where her fellow University students went to score their "shit". The place was packed solid, Clarence Carter's 'Patches' booming out of the jukebox as we queued at the bar, and I noticed that it was more ethnically diverse than most pubs in the town centre at that time and possibly why my girlfriend was drawn to it, being of Chinese Trinidadian origin. I remember looking around furtively and detecting no visible signs of drug dealing, but then I wouldn't have had the slightest idea what that would have looked like anyway. I only became aware of it some years later when I accompanied two groupies who'd come down for the Festival and were on their way to meet up with a member of Bad Company but wanted to score some pills first. I remember feeling very exposed as the transaction was conducted with the minimum of stealth in the middle of the main bar. My point is that the place had established a certain reputation long before punk arrived.

Today, an energetic and enthusiastic Facebook page celebrates the pub in what is now considered its heyday: the late 70s and early 80s. The principle punk hangout, it was where you met prior to a gig, or to cadge a lift if said gig was out of town, or just to hang out with other members of your tribe. General Accident regarded it as their HQ and, in Nod's words, "owned the back bar". He remarked that it was where you went to get your dope, which was also what young punk Mick Brock picked up on too, noting that it had a rough feel about it. No wonder ex-Oratory School pupil Stuart Osbourne realised after a drink there that, despite his best efforts, he was still a middle-class boy through and through. As was a young Basingstoke girl with multiple piercings and peroxide hair who used to hang out occasionally and was referred to as Posh Liz. Yep, fooling around with Hugh Grant was definitely a step down for her.

Opposite page: The Star on Duke Street, viewed from the Lower Ship Hotel bar entrance

Trash, but by name only

Trash were already on their way up when Nick Duckett booked them for the opening night of his new venue, The Garage. Initially a student band formed in Weybridge, a lucky break got them recommended to a bloke with his own production company and they wound up signed to Polydor Records. Woah! That's quite a break, but then they were a good-looking bunch and their first single, 'Priorities', is quite a debut. It rocks like crazy and is stuffed full of 1977's curled lip snarl. It was a terrific start and deserved to be huge. Sadly, it didn't sell, although it picked up substantial airplay and some good reviews in the national music press.

Their move to Reading brought them a new drummer, Brian Devoil, sometime manager of Clayson and The Argonauts, and plenty of gigs, including supporting punk favourites 999 at the University's Fresher's Ball, along with regular appearances at Bones and, of course, The Target.

In Nick Duckett's review of the band's performance in his garage, er, I mean, in The Garage, where they played two encores to an ecstatic crowd, he had this to say about them:

> "If the band are to overcome the obstacle of the fact that they seem to have no marketable image at present they could well go far".

N-N-E-R-V-O-U-S, the Trash single produced by Shel Talmy

Shortly afterwards they began appearing on stage dressed and illuminated in stark, blinding white. Image sorted. And commenting on an appearance at Bones early in the new year fanzine Kiss This said much that was positive about the boys whilst sounding a warning to punters:

> "no way are these boys punk so don't expect them to be... their set is composed of catchy melodies and good old rock and roll... and if Power Pop... is this year's big thing... then these boys should do alright."

With another new drummer, Simon Butler-Smith on board, the band were offered another opportunity their rivals might have killed for; to record with Shel Talmy, legendary producer of early classics by The Who and The Kinks. The resulting single, 'N-N-E-R-V-O-U-S', is an absolute corker and in the same tradition as the aforementioned but again failed to sell in the quantities it deserved. At least Pete Townshend liked it, telling them so when they failed the audition to be the in-house band for the film *Quadrophenia*, which must have been some consolation anyway.

Trash typically performed dressed in stark white

And that was kinda that. But there was much to be proud of. They were there almost from the start, released a couple of excellent singles, recorded with a legend, were reviewed favourably and consistently in the national press, had a fan club and, for a time, their own version of Hawkwind's Stacia dancing with them on stage. A class act.

The K9s

Mr Ian Aird, known as Sprog for as far back as anyone can remember, bought a guitar with only four strings and took it into his school in Crowthorne where happily somebody pointed out to him that what he'd bought was in fact a bass guitar. He decided to learn to play it. Being the only bassist in school meant he was much in demand, eventually teaming up with three lads in the year below him, Kevin, Greg and Rick. Guitarist Greg reckoned he knew about ten chords which in the musical climate of 1977 made him a virtuoso. They became Ricky Rodent and the Sewer Rats for their first gig at Crowthorne Village Hall, hired a P.A. and turned it up so loud it nearly emptied the place. Sprog says

> "we were just soaking it all up. To us punk was all about having some fun."

Soon known as The K9s they quickly established themselves at Bones, playing on the same ten-hour Bank Holiday punkathon as The Lurkers in March 1978. The reviewer for the Evening Post was impressed, fanzine Kiss This even more so:

> "This band are so shit-hot that after the gig there is steam billowing out of the bogs."

Much of their material consisted of just changing the lyrics to well-known songs and playing them faster. As Sprog says today, they wrote material the way a sixteen-year-old would when drunk. Mostly quite rude, I'm not going to give you any examples here, ok?

They played fast, high-energy music infused with anarchic humour, the very definition of one strand of punk, the local area's Damned to General Accident's Clash. But a record release was required if they were going to make any progress. In typical fashion, one of the tracks for the impending release was written in the back of a taxi on the way to the studio, Woodcray, in Wokingham, where on arrival they found all these drunk punks ready to do their bit as backing vocalists. The studio staff were not amused.

And the gigs were always lively affairs, the enthusiasm of the fans and the anarchic playfulness of the band ensuring that. A Wokingham Rock Club appearance, or non-appearance as it turned out, resulted in a near-riot as fans fought running battles with what Sprog termed "smoothie elements". They had been booked as support to a metal band who promptly pulled out, taking their P.A. with them, when faced with K9s' punk stormtroopers. Similar tales still do the rounds

K9s gig poster

with the action centred around Forest School, Fairmile Hospital, The Paradise Club supporting The Angelic Upstarts and even The Target. They were getting banned a lot, their supporters just a bit too lively for most club owners' likes and the lads decided to call it a day. But this certainly wasn't the last we heard of Greg, Sprog, Kevin and Rick.

The Romantix

Rob Rose should have been a big star. Possessor of a fine voice and the writer of many absurdly catchy pop songs, it just didn't happen for him the way it should have done. It was certainly not for the lack of a decent band behind him though, because The Romantix were a superb combo. A lack of flash in the volatile age of punk? Possibly, but I'm scratching about here for possible excuses.

Except for local country-music legend Terry Clarke, Rob was the smartest dresser in town, and a man transformed by having witnessed a performance by the outstanding Curtis Mayfield at The Top Rank. He was encouraged in his ambitions by his art teacher at Ashmead, Roger Barnes, vocalist with that marvellous collection of local rhythm and blues talent known as Motley Crew.

Recruiting Steve Hampson and Henry Smithson on guitar and bass respectively, and ex-Trash drummer Simon Butler-Smith, rehearsals were held in the basement of the vicarage in Peppard where Butler-Smith's father was the incumbent. Emerging into the light in 1978 their gigs were organised by the dynamic duo of Rich Roberts and Geoff Benson on an expenses-only arrangement. Formerly successful entertainment bookers for Bulmershe College they recognised talent when they saw it.

Gigs ranged across the South of England, and locally included Bones and The Target, obviously. Possibly their most prestigious appearance was at The Music Machine in Camden supporting Swindon's Stadium Dogs. Or maybe it was the Mod Night, held at the nightclub Heaven, under the arches at Charing Cross. A photograph shows them dancing on the roof of the Transit that night. Just happy to be playing in a great band, I expect. They were a perfect fit for the emerging Mod scene. Both the look of the boys, and their music and lyrics were grounded in the 60s sounds of The Who and The Action, the era reflected in a lot of Rob's songs, like 'Brighton Beaches', and 'Sixteen'. Bassist Henry Smithson describes Rob's songs as having "the energy of punk and the New Wave but with better tunes and more memorable melodic and lyrical hooks."

And as for their live performances he goes on to say that

"when we played live we didn't hold back. Every gig we did we just went for it. People responded to that."

Lasting only a couple of years their final appearance at Reading Tech was, by all accounts, magnificent, with the band breaking up on a high. Support that night came from the up and coming Between Pictures, fronted by Alison Rolls who was later to became Rob's partner until his sadly premature death in 2014. If you want to understand how good a band The Romantix were check out the reggae-inflected track 'Honey You're In My Head' and the sheer Mod exuberance of 'Sixteen' and marvel to the sound of a Reading outfit that should have been massive. But this was just the first chapter in his story, as the recordings with his musical vehicle in the 80s, Red For Go, attest to. Sparkling with energy, they fill the listener with a sense that this guy knew just how to soundtrack the good times.

The Romantix gig posters

The Lemon Kittens

This was a band that was never going to make it easy for the listener. Formed in Reading by Karl Blake and Gary Thatcher in 1977, early appearances at the University also included Danielle Dax, who designed the cover for their unsettlingly titled EP, *Spoonfed and Writhing*. The opening track was a cover of Brit rock and roller Johnny Kidd's classic, 'Shaking All Over', as if recalled from a nightmare. With The Flying Lizards scoring a hit around this time with a minimalist take on the R'n'B classic, 'Money', there was something of a move by experimentalists to dissect and re-examine the musical bedrocks of popular culture. The Kittens, however, kept elements of their sound solidly grounded within a punk framework, the tortured, spiky guitar keeping faith with the movement's origins.

Never destined to be a big draw, perhaps, their musical adventuring nonetheless registered nationally and even internationally, something others in the town were struggling to achieve. This was punk music at the edge of creation and was never going to find a warm welcome in either The Target or Cherry's Wine Bar, but they were just passing through anyway.

Dax joined the crew, but Hatcher seems to have jumped ship for the recording of the creepily titled LP, *We Buy A Hammer For Daddy*, in 1980. Now working firmly within the orbit of Captain Beefheart's brain-squeezing epic, *Trout Mask Replica*, there are also revealing touches of Ivor Cutler's eccentricity, in-your-face punk aggression and even shades of heavy metal. It's the sound of enquiringly dark imaginations having a ball with sound, but it is also hard to digest after about ten minutes exposure to the creators' twisted visions. A further single and album followed, *(Those Who Bite The Hand That Feeds Them Must Sooner Or Later Meet The) Big Dentist*. Gulp! And they went their separate ways, Blake to the Shock-Headed Peters, Dax to a highly regarded and internationally successful solo career continuing to cultivate the alarming image of a psychotic Miss Havisham. The Kittens' music still sounds fresh, still sounds original, and will forever remain challenging.

Opposite page: Danielle Dax, and the abum cover for 'Spoonfed + Writhing' designed by her

3. The Good Times are Just Around the Corner

Rehearsing

If you had been excited by the overwhelmingly negative reaction that punk sparked amongst your elder siblings, your parents, your teachers and most of your classmates then there was a fair chance you were eager to sign on and do your bit for the cause.

You may have been inspired by punk's up-and-at-'em, do-it-yourself attitude, but that didn't necessarily mean that you wanted to sound or even look like a punk band. Take Waingels pupil Baz Barry for example, whose attitude and approach to music pre-dated the punk explosion and like Lemmy with Motörhead, just seemed to fit right in with it. Not coming from a musical family, he had no idea how he'd go about emulating the people he saw every week on his favourite TV show, 'Top of the Pops'. But one day his science teacher picked up a guitar at the end of a lesson and strummed out what Baz recognised instantly as a Status Quo riff. He was spellbound, and it didn't look too difficult. Obviously, he'd need a guitar. He borrowed the necessaries, picked up a cheap second-hand number and was proudly carrying this prized possession home when disaster struck. He takes up the story:

> "There was this good-looking girl coming the other way and as we passed this dodgy tremolo arm dropped off the guitar and it all fell apart with a loud twaaaang! I just knew from that moment that I would have a glorious career in music!"

His band Predatür's energy and commitment ensured for them a seamless passage into this frantic new musical universe.

> "'God Save the Queen!' That song still makes the goosebumps go up on the back of my neck."

It was no problem staging your initial rehearsals in your bedroom but as soon as you cranked up the volume you had a problem, and testing the tolerance of your neighbours once too often was likely to end badly. The Reading Evening Post ran a story about a group of

The very collectable Predatür single released by Quicksilver in 1982

young punks from Woodley calling themselves, appropriately enough, Out Of Order, who'd been banned from their street for being too noisy. A parent was appealing on their behalf for a safe space where they could whack up the amps to eleven.

Church and Community Halls could be booked cheaply but were not, of course, soundproof, and a band could find that their initial booking was also their last. One Reading band, settled for the evening in a remote Village Hall, had their rehearsal abruptly terminated because the caretaker had received several calls from irate householders several miles distant concerning the bloody awful racket being made. At least the guilty party had found a suitable name for their band: The Complaints From Burghfield Common, later shortened for commercial reasons!

Today, most towns have professional-standard rehearsal facilities, but back in the late 70s such places were rare indeed. I bought my first house on the strength of it having a cellar that could be used as a rehearsal space. In no time at all it ended up being booked out every night of the week to aspiring local acts, there being few alternatives. It was a noisy place to live, the primitive soundproofing acting only to absorb the racket in this tiny space, provoking the musicians to keep turning up the volume. Unwitting visitors risked serious aural trauma, frankly.

Things started to improve by the early 80s when ex-General Accident and -Crooks bassist Chris Broderick started renting out space in his property next to Central Swimming Pool, and in the mid-80s ex-Geisha Girls drummer Danny Fraifeld set up a series of rooms above a taxi business in Cheapside and found himself running the operation twenty-four hours a day just to cope with the demand, before moving the operation to Cemetery Junction.

Some bands never got any further than the rehearsal stage, for many others it was enough just to appear at a friend's birthday party or the end of year school concert. For most though, that first appearance brought such a thrill they just had to have more. Just ask Richard Seymour of the enigmatically named Erik Stig Band. A job in the late 70s brought Richard to Reading and a post five-a-side competition pint revealed enough musical talent in the team to form a band, subsequent rehearsals taking place in the work's canteen where they were adoringly watched by a cleaner, in their eyes their one and only groupie.

Inspired by the mighty Spizzenergi's single, 'Where's Captain Kirk?', they quickly progressed from playing covers to writing their own material, a move that automatically transforms you from just being a "covers" band into serious musical contenders, or so most combos believe. The gigs now followed; the works' Xmas Do, a self-promotion at Sonning Village Hall with the band's ranks swollen by the addition of two backing singers, Cherry's Wine Bar, the University Battle of the Bands Competition, the long and winding road...

Sadly, it didn't turn into the hoped-for five-year mission, work and life in general getting in the way. But it all made such an impression on him that forty years later he has this piece of advice for anyone considering giving it a go:

"Go for it! You'll never have so much fun ever again."

Recording

Your newly formed combo was bound to have captured a rehearsal on cassette. Obviously, the sheer thrill of hearing yourselves playing live quickly led to a sense of dissatisfaction with the quality of sound achieved on such basic equipment. By the early 80s porta-studio technology allowed the lucky owner to record on a bog-standard cassette as many individual tracks (4) as The Beatles had when recording 'Sgt. Pepper's Lonely Hearts Club Band', but right here, in your bedroom, whilst wearing headphones. They didn't come cheap, though. No, if you wanted studio quality you were going to have to book yourself into a proper studio and the small, local set-ups

Red for Go cassette

which started to multiply towards the end of the 70s would cost you around a hundred pounds for the time it took to record and mix four well-rehearsed tracks. You'd have the expertise of the owner/recording engineer thrown in, a fresh cassette of the result for each expectant band member and the ingestion of a limitless supply of caffeine. Roll-ups extra, of course.

As well as being a rites-of-passage event for your band, you needed some concrete evidence of your musical worth to secure bookings, although frankly, any publican who valued their reputation would do their homework and at least ask around a bit before agreeing to a booking, but a tape would certainly help.

Besides, a decent recording was something that you could offer your hopefully growing number of fans. Ace university crew Twelfth Night, musically as far removed from punk as was humanly possible, utilised this DIY punk approach very successfully indeed, producing three cassette-only releases early in their stellar career which they then sold at gigs or offered fans via mail-order.

And yes, you'd send a copy of your much-prized musical masterpiece to all the major, and minor, record labels whilst kind of suspecting that they would probably end up as landfill, unheard. Another ex-Bulmershe social secretary who later worked as a talent spotter for a major international record company, did just that with a tape from a Birmingham-based combo he'd just rejected. If only they'd sent a photograph, he mused later, having missed the opportunity to sign Duran Duran.

There were, however, some people out there in positions of influence who might just give you a break. Step forward that tireless champion of punk, John Peel, who'd occasionally play demo tapes on his Radio 1 show. 'Teenage Kicks' by The Undertones, reputedly his all-time favourite song, first aired to listeners on his *Top Gear* show as a demo tape. A short time later we had our own radio stars doing a similar job in the Thames Valley, of whom more later.

There was a fair selection of relatively affordable studios within a short Transit journey of central Reading just waiting for your business. Audiogenic, formerly Sun Studios, was situated in Crown Street and had boasted the first eight-track set-up outside London. It had punk credentials too, having worked with both The Vibrators and XTC. Not every session went according to plan, of course. Local

Grinding Halt issue 12 and the Sub-Active flexi disc give-away

fanzine impresario Stuart Osbourne, aka Eddie Snide, recorded tracks there with his band Sub Active for a flexi disc to be given away with what turned out to be the final edition of his wonderful publication *Grinding Halt*. It didn't go well, but with deadlines imminent, they decided to press ahead with the release of what is now an extremely collectable artefact:

> "We knew it was a crock of shit and begged our readers to give us another chance. It was our first time in the studio. The guitar and bass are in tune, just not with each other."

Actually, it's not that bad.

Chris Broderick's Matinee Music on the Oxford Road was popular with everybody on the local scene, not least because of the knowledge and band experience of the man himself. Still going today, it is now a much-respected specialised set up for multilingual voice-over work.

Alan Clayson, John Townsend and Dave Berry at Woodcray, 1986

Doug Gleave's competitively priced studio in Wokingham was popular with first timers, having a reputation for getting the best out of the understandably nervous and inexperienced. However, it was also the studio in which those prog innovators Twelfth Night recorded their first commercially available tape.

Martin Nichols' terraced house set-up was also in Wokingham. Known as The Basement it was widely regarded as the best going. Cramped, but relaxed and friendly, bands returned time after time to work with this dedicated, friendly and supremely talented producer and engineer, so that when he upped sticks and moved the organisation to larger premises in Weston Super Mare and became The White House Studio his client base were more than happy to travel down for a session by the sea. They still are. His work with the likes of Reading's genre-defining trailblazers Slowdive at the end of the 80s was instrumental in helping to launch that band's music into the rock stratosphere and the appreciation of a globally receptive audience.

And everybody wanted to record at Woodcray, located in former farm buildings in Wokingham. In the early 80s it offered a step up to the dizzying heights of complexity with sixteen separate tracks but was consequently considerably more expensive. It was also a roomier and more comfortable environment to work in and gave access to the latest in programmable digital drum technology when this state-of-the-art stuff was still prohibitively expensive. It was just an illusion, of course, but recording there made you feel like you were making progress as a band, somehow. And you tended to be well-rehearsed on arrival, The K9s being a notable exception to this, to avoid wasting your own money and the excellent engineer Nick Horne's time. Black Sabbath recorded an album there in the mid-80s and could probably have afforded to be a bit more relaxed about costs.

If you could get somebody else to stump up the money for recording, so much the better. James Carter, later of The Soft Dogs, was a member of local heavy metal outfit, Firebird. Purley resident, legendary Deep Purple vocalist Ian Gillan, had offered a day in his own studio, Kingsway, as the prize in a local fete raffle. Won by a fellow school student, twenty-five pounds changed hands, and Firebird had their ticket to ride, meeting up with Mr Gillan at The Roebuck in Tilehurst for preliminaries.

The outcome? A privately pressed, limited edition single which, due to the Gillan connection, is cited in various NWBHM books as integral to that scene's development. Gillan even came to see them play Emmer Green Youth Club and signed a few copies. Oh, and if you're looking to own a copy, I should start saving now!

4. Punk Goes to College, Reluctantly

The Barbarians are at the Gate

When The Sex Pistols performed for the Fine Art Department on the old London Road campus in June 1976 they drew an audience of just twenty people, few people outside London being in the know at that time. But by January 1977 punk had developed into an authentic working-class youth cult that was both as frightening and as disconcerting as working-class skinheads had been to hippies. And since part of being a punk was to unsettle the established order, many embraced the wearing of Nazi regalia and joyfully indulged in the alarming habit of gobbing all over their musical heroes, a nasty, but thankfully short-lived habit that Mic Dover describes from the time his band, Between Pictures, supported the real deal, 999, at the Marquee Club:

> "We walked on stage to see a tsunami of spittle hurtling towards us through the stage lights... I looked down to see long strands of green-tinted gob glistening across my guitar strings!"

This sort of thing was never going to go down well on campus. In fact, most further education establishments were understandably nervous about booking acts whose music seemed to be linked to such alarmingly anti-social behaviour.

This would all change as confidence, familiarity and the popularity of the music grew, but in those first months of 1977 promotions at the University and Bulmershe proceeded as if nothing much had happened, with just one or two notable exceptions.

Reading University's student newspaper, *Shell*, once again proved to be an invaluable source of information regarding musical events on campus, when it was published, that is, and this seems not to have been the case for most of 1977. Up and running again for the autumn term it was by this time beginning to resemble the *New Musical Express*, demonstrating the central place that popular music's ever-changing style held for students. Dominated as they were by the middle classes, punk may have come across like a slap in the face for most undergraduates in the early days, but the sheer exuberance of the music and the wave of creativity that it unleashed

Between Pictures supporting 999 at the Marquee Club, 1979

transformed the live music experience on campus and the attitude of all but the most determined traditionalists.

The day following The Vibrators' appearance at Bulmershe in early March the University's presentation of traditional rockers, The Pat Travers Band, already looked like an anachronism. In support, however, were those proto-punk art rockers The Doctors of Madness who'd played the University as recently as December. It was a gentle way to dip your toes into the new wave, so to speak, although The Doctors found themselves out in the cold less than a year later, already yesterday's news, a fate that overtook many a class act in the wake of the punk apocalypse. Not so Squeeze, who appeared a couple of weeks later and featured the now-very-famous Jools Holland. Shiny and new, but never punk, they were saved by the quality of their songwriting and the breadth of their appeal. They played short, sharp, tuneful material with inspired lyrics that you could dance to, and that helped a lot. Having The Damned play the student union at the end of March would have been an entirely different matter, however, had it taken place. They were booked for the 30th but cried off, citing exhaustion after returning from their

Tom Robinson Band's debut single 2-4-6-8 Motorway was a top five hit on the UK Singles Chart in 1977.

first US tour. In fact, they were playing on the Continent at this time and had perhaps been offered a better deal.

   The University's Summer Ball in June was headlined by the excellent Kursaal Flyers, so recently the darlings of the college circuit but doomed like The Doctors to die within the year. The Troggs were also on the bill, perhaps the UK's only true garage band, having found that their three-chord 60s chart toppers were fashionable again. A nod in the direction of changing times saw punk new boys 999 complete the bill. They came back for the Fresher's Ball in the early autumn, the reviews in *Shell* for this appearance being decidedly mixed. They reveal a definite student antagonism towards the new music, although one reviewer seemed about to be won over:

> "I thought 999 were good and I am by no means one of the bin-liner and safety pin set."

Ah, bless him, and no reports of flying spittle either.
Supported by the Borough's newest residents Trash the sound mix in the hall was apparently terrible and both bands would probably have been better off playing the bar.

A packed autumn schedule included The Tom Robinson Band, who's single '2-4-6-8 Motorway' had just made the Top 10. An excellent and much-loved combo, they helped to change the face of sexual politics in the UK with extraordinary songs like 'Glad To Be Gay', sung with gusto by gig-goers across the land. They were never punk but flourished in punk's wake, their appearances attracting a mixed audience of rock and punk fans demonstrating the tolerance and inclusivity of the emerging scene.

They were supported by Birmingham boys Suburban Studs, who were dismissed by *Shell's* reviewer as "Middle of the road new wavers." This is a patronising student put-down of a youthful, energetic, working-class combo who were anything but middle of the road, his undoubted prejudice revealed by the following comment:

> "punk music is self-destructive and is on the way out.
> 1978 promises the return of pure pop rock."

Well, the music was never going to stand still. These were restless and exciting times and pure pop rock was certainly on the menu for the following year, but it wasn't yet the end for all that chaos and anarchy so enthusiastically and recently embraced.

Early 1978 saw the University stage a reggae triple-header, with UK rising stars Steel Pulse heading the bill and a show that was favourably received by the lads from the *Kiss This* fanzine who even managed to blag a backstage interview with the Birmingham crew. Punk and reggae would appear to have been poles apart musically, but the huge influence that reggae was to have in shaping punk's future was just around the corner and would help to transform it from being much more than just an angry howl of rage, impressive as that was in the right hands, into something more focused, danceable and, frankly, more commercial. And a realisation on the part of punks that however tough they found things to be at the end of the 70s, being black in the UK made life a whole lot harder.

With The Sex Pistols rapidly disintegrating, Jimmy Pursey became, mercifully briefly, the voice of a generation. As lead singer with Sham 69 he lapped up the attention as the band secured three top ten hits in just over a year. They appeared at both Bulmershe College and the Tech in early 1978 and once again those newshounds for the fanzine *Kiss This* were on the case, interviewing Pursey before he took to the Bulmershe stage:

> "The commies don't know what to make of me and neither do the NF, coz I'm against all types of politics. I just wanna have a laugh."

By the time they played the Festival in August this band of late-coming rabble rousers had acquired the fan base they so richly deserved, the NF supporting skinheads who'd gathered to see them causing violent mayhem. To his credit, Pursey seemed visibly upset that day and must have realised he'd awoken a monster. I only hope the two college gigs went more smoothly.

At the other end of the punk scale Planet Gong, soon to be known as Here and Now, packed out the Tech refectory with all-comers. These commune-living, hippy-looking, ethereal-sounding, hallucinogenic-loving men and women always played for free, relying on a voluntary collection to keep their wagons rolling. Their mistrust of the capitalist way of doing things chimed with Mark Perry, creator of the original punk fanzine, *Sniffin' Glue*, and leader of punk pioneers and musical boundary-stretchers Alternative TV, who shared an LP with them the following year, one side each. He'd have felt a lot closer to them as a punk than to Sham 69, I imagine.

At the University, old-stagers like The Strawbs, The Kinks and Slade continued to deliver entertainment commensurate with their sizeable booking fees, and The Pleasers confirmed that pop rock was indeed becoming huge this year, although *Shell's* reviewer was a bit sniffy about them:

> "Four smiling moptop impersonators decked out in neat matching blue/grey suits and red ties."

And creating an atmosphere akin to a Young Conservatives disco, apparently.

Gang of Four: Gigs at the Town Hall and the University by this Leeds combo were a big influence on the Reading scene.

They also presented a performance by the hugely influential Gang of Four, whose industrial-sounding funky sparseness came all the way down from Leeds by way of Cologne. Their performance was an inspiration to so many who attended, suggesting to all who heard them an alternative direction of travel for punk-inspired music.

Not so The Fabulous Poodles. Booked by the University for the not inconsiderable sum of £500, someone pointed out to ENTS that this was a band notorious for their use of inappropriate stage banter and for their misogynistic, sexualised song lyrics. According to Shell's

TOYAH
THE BIRD IN FLIGHT TOUR

JANUARY		FEBRUARY	
Friday 18th STAFFORD	North Staffs Poly College	Friday 1st LONDON	South Bank Poly
Saturday 19th HITCHIN	College	Saturday 2nd READING	Bulmershe College
Sunday 20th LONDON	Marquee	Tuesday 5th TORQUAY	400 Club
Thursday 24th BLACKPOOL	Norbreck Castle	Thursday 7th PORT TALBOT	Troubadour
Friday 25th HUDDERSFIELD	Poly	Friday 8th HARROW	Technical College
Sunday 27th LEEDS	Fan Club at Branigans	Saturday 9th LONDON	Music Machine
Monday 28th DONCASTER	Romeo & Juliet		
Tuesday 29th NOTTINGHAM	Trent Poly		
Thursday 31st NORWICH	St Andrews Hall		

New Double 'A' Side Single
BIRD IN FLIGHT   **TRIBAL LOOK**

SAFE 22

Toyah's Bird in Flight tour took her to Bulmershe College on 2 February 1980.

reporter howls of protest broke out across campus, foremost among them being Reading's Women's Group, who felt it necessary to

"Object to the denigration of women in such songs as 'Tit Photographer Blues', and 'Topless Go-Go Dancer', which labour under the illusion that women are brainless statistics."

Mindful of the Union policy that "opposes the promotion of activities which specifically exploit the female sex" ENTS were left with no choice but to cancel the engagement, although, it being rather late in the day, they lost their five-hundred-pound booking fee. Good to

Twelfth Night gig flyer

see that matters relating to sexual politics were debated as fiercely back then as they are today.

Soon to be massive acts like Adam and the Ants posed no problems though, nor Toyah or Judie Tzuke who were both booked to perform at Bulmershe as the 70s ended. But what was particularly noticeable by then was just how much local talent was muscling in on the college action. Among these pioneers were Motley Crew, Double Xposure, The Romantix, A Fast Crowd, Twelfth Night, El Seven and The Great Mistakes, all of them now reaching out to new audiences beyond the clubs and bars of the town centre.

Reaching for the Stars

Unsigned local acts got to play the Student's Union bar, the coffee lounge and the various halls of residence on a regular basis, but not often the Main Hall, which was generally the preserve of those artists capable of selling fifteen hundred tickets. Mind you, they were in good company. U2 played in the bar in November 1980 less than a month after the release of their first LP, Boy. The place was packed solid according to Mick Brock, grateful ever since for having caught them so early in their monstrously successful career. So, who got to choose the acts who played the Main Hall? Two former University social secretaries put us in the picture:

> "So, you have a couple of grand to spend. You've got to pay security, print posters, tickets etc and that's six hundred gone. Allow for VAT, work out your capacity and then work back to the ticket price. Oh, and book artists your fellow students want to see, not necessarily just on artistic merit."

This pitch in a job interview on graduating with a lower second in quantity surveying secured Jez Dyer the position he was after, his prospective employers clearly seeing that here was someone who could run a business but didn't yet realise it, all thanks to the three years he spent organising entertainment at the University as part of the ENTS team in the early 80s.

As did Neil Richards a year or two later. By his own admission a real stickler for health and safety, he'd test every fire door and post security at vulnerable points, taking the habit into his post-university days promoting shows at the After Dark Club, the Trades Union Club and a sold out and fondly remembered appearance by The Stone Roses at The Majestic.

Being part of ENTS was a time-consuming business that was undertaken alongside the student's regular studies, and if the complaints to *Shell* about various promotions are to be taken at face value then the ENTS people were on a hiding to nothing. So why would you do it? Neil explains:

> "I used to stand in the balcony of the Main Hall looking at a sell-out crowd of fifteen hundred having a good time and think, I caused this to happen. It's a good feeling."

Both signed up to ENTS during Fresher's week and found that for the first year they were doing all the odd jobs like running errands for the artists; the position of social secretary, head of publicity or treasurer being taken in the second year. The third year was all about trying to secure a half-decent degree after all the time missed during the second!

Jez had a bit of luck with his first promotion, the Fresher's Ball, and it set him up for the rest of the year. Estimating that most freshers would have been in their early teens when this man was an almost constant fixture on *Top of the Pops*, he booked the now-disgraced Gary Glitter, even then desperate to get his career back on track, for what Jez considered a modest fee upfront and no percentage of the door take. The performance sold out in no time and the money made that night allowed Jez to take a few risks with his promotions for the rest of the year. Mind you, a list that included the likes of New Order, The Thompson Twins, Tears for Fears, Level 42, Bauhaus, Public Image and Imagination look sure-fire winners from here.

You learned fast on the job, and dealing with musicians was not always easy. Neil tells of the time he booked New Order and they refused to sign a contract, happy just to have a verbal agreement

Jez Dyer's NUS card 1982–83

between parties. Anxious to the point of exhaustion that they would renege on this, they not only arrived on time but delivered a triumphant show. They had in the meantime been offered a booking in Holland for four times the money for the same date but, according to one of the road crew, turned it down to play the University. Respect! It helped, according to Jez, that the bands and the students were all around the same age and that the artists weren't dealing with some nasty corporate organisation, although ex-Sex Pistol John Lydon arrived with his band Public Image and took exception to the fact that Jez was wearing the same jacket as him! And Neil was looking forward to presenting one of his musical heroes, Terry Hall, formerly of The Specials. Unusually, he demanded to be paid in advance and then gave a lack-lustre performance that was short, encore-less and laced with insults to both the audience and the venue:

"This song has made me two hundred and fifty thousand dollars, which means I shouldn't have to play shit gigs like this."

Never meet your heroes, thought Neil philosophically.

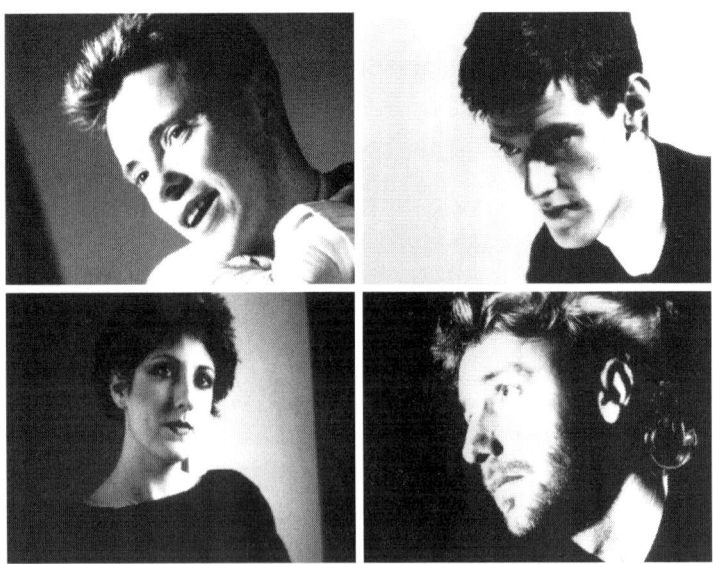

New Order

5. Let's Put the Show on Right Here!

Just Do It Yourself

You've formed a band, but so far the only people who have seen you in action are your long-suffering partners and your mum. They all love you, but you know full well that objective criticism will only come when you are standing in front of a bunch of indifferent strangers who might even have paid money for the privilege. It's time to get out there and face them.

You could take the very pro-active route to live performance, like future Howlin' Horror Denny Mills, a man who'd been inspired by the true rock and roll greats, wanting to sing like Little Richard, play like Jerry Lee Lewis and write songs like Buddy Holly. He'd also cut his teeth performing Bob Dylan numbers in folk clubs under the mentorship of two of Reading's own musical legends, Mike Cooper and Terry Clarke. Along with his brother Dave on bass these two self-schooled rock and rollers were all set to let loose a touch of 50s mayhem on the new scene and remind the world where all

Denny Mills rehearsing with the Howlin' Horrors

this teenage angst had originated, performing under the very apt moniker of The Rock and Roll Dazzlers. Working days as a printer, Denny had acquired a van and a small PA system. The boys would scour Yellow Pages for the addresses of local youth clubs and then turn up unannounced, set up and play for free. They must have been quite impressive. Denny remembers that

> "People used to ask for our autographs. I used to say, can I have yours then?"

They were as inspired by punk's get-up-and-go attitude as Baz was with his Quo-inspired crew Predatür. For their debut they booked Woodcote Village Hall, figuring that with so little to do of an evening in that neck of the woods they'd fill it easily. They were right. They'd also had a piece of luck. Chick Churchill of Ten Years After lived near Goring and after a chance encounter offered to lend the boys some equipment. They must have looked like the real deal as they took to the stage that night in front of banks of professional-standard equipment, albeit with the name of one of the biggest stars of Woodstock stencilled all over the back. Predatür's performance was

Predatür on stage at The Target in 1980

a triumph that night, a triumph they repeated in the same location a couple of weeks later.

In the guise of his alter-ego Mordecai Smyth, ex-Waingels pupil Ian Mundwyler has three acclaimed 21st-century psych long players to his credit, having picked up at the age of fifteen an album by Syd Barrett that sent him tumbling head-first down that rabbit hole into a world where punk and psychedelia amount to much the same thing. However, the first band he joined had the same sexual composition as Abba and similar musical ambitions.

Feeling that the time had come to face the music, so to speak, they booked Woodley Players Theatre, a venue that had never before staged musical events but was prepared to give it a go, and enthusiastically set about selling every ticket, a job made easier by teaming up with a couple of other hopeful first-timers. The combined totals of family, friends and friends of friends managed to do the trick, and so well did the evening go, and so buoyed-up their confidence, they repeated the trick a few months later.

Perhaps even more successful was a booking to play for a lunch-break fashion show at The Majestic where they were asked if they

A young Ian Mundwyler displays his punk credentials

could perform in the intervals when the models were changing. Indeed they could, and the experience turned into something of an eye-opener for Ian, unused as he was to the sight of so many young women constantly stripping off to change into their next outfit right in front of him!

Eventually deciding that he didn't really like Abba after all, Ian quit, feeling that the time had come in his musical development to exorcise his inner goth.

Everybody's seen *School of Rock*, right? Jack Black's character forms a band with a bunch of posh eight -year-olds who then go on and win a Battle of the Bands competition. They were popular, tacky, compulsive affairs and often a spur to newly formed combos to get on and go seize the day. The cynicism inherent within the punk scene should have killed them off. It did, but it was a lingering death.

The University had been staging such shows annually for years, the jamborees becoming increasingly well organised over time although much of the entertainment still came from those acts who'd obviously just entered for a dare. This certainly wasn't the case at the Hexagon in 1978 when a contest organised by local independent station Radio 210 and hosted by two of their own, Steve Wright and "Whispering" Bob Harris, dissolved into chaos as fans of General Accident did more than just voice their displeasure at their heroes' third place. The trouble rather overshadowed the class of the winning act, Hazzard, a popular local hard rock outfit who'd been packing out The Target for some time. I guess all's fair in love and local band competitions.

A couple of years later another of these shindigs was held at the Top Rank, a series of heats culminating in a grand finale, the contestants including myself playing with The Complaints. It was our first ever live performance and somehow or other we made it through to the final. Presumably the organisers assumed that each act would bring coachloads of fans, but since for most of us this was only our first or second public appearance there gaped this vast, empty space in front of the stage, the few paying customers clustered around the bar at the back of the hall. God bless those few intrepid souls who crossed that empty void and jigged about in support. We didn't win, the worthy recipients being Yateley's own pin-smart rockers Blind Date, but we felt exhilarated to have survived and had even left the stage to some polite applause. Next stop, Cherry's Wine Bar....

Open Your own Club, With In Hill House

The Upper Deck in Bridge Street is a wonderfully self-contained venue at the top of a flight of stairs overlooking The Kennet and used extensively as a jazz club during the 60s and 70s. Given a good dusting off for the 80s it found a new lease of life as The Hermit Club around 1984. Open every Wednesday night, one band appeared very regularly indeed. They were In Hill House, and this may have been because their management team had opened the club specifically to provide a regular and controllable environment in which they could present their proteges to the world.

A good-looking foursome, they played and sang well enough and had a kind of cheeky-sweet stage persona and a whole bunch of half decent songs, as evidenced by their management-released single, 'Sanctuary'. And they pulled in a sizeable and almost fanatical crowd for every one of their performances at the top of that flight of stairs, their following largely composed of enthusiastic and excitable teenage girls.

Local fanzine *Utterance*, for whom this blatantly commercial-sounding record was not at all to their taste suggested that the record

> "could be played by Steve Wright or Gary Davies and no one would notice! It could be hyped onto *Top of the Pops* and the Duranies (fans of Duran Duran presumably) would be sure to sing along."

At least they'd spotted the record's commercial possibilities, as had the band's management, and they were keen to take things to the next level, so they hatched a plan.

They hired The Complaints' sound system and two of us to operate it, guitarist Richard and myself. It was then loaded onto a flat-bed truck and driven up to London, the idea being that the band would play live outside as many major recording company offices as possible to try and secure a deal. Parked a block away, the sound system was fired up and the band clambered aboard, launching into their first number just as the truck took up a position in front of the head office of Virgin, EMI, Island or whoever was next on the list.

Within seconds every window in whichever Central London square we were in flew open and workers crowded to see just what the hell was going on out there. Sadly, on each occasion the band had very little time to impress before somebody with obvious authority quickly emerged and took the band's management to one side for a little chat. That, or the police arrived. The general response seemed to be, well done lads! Really, it was like The Beatles on that Savile Row rooftop all over again. Sort of.

After several stops, Virgin Records invited them in to record something straight away, bringing this travelling roadshow to a close. And no, it didn't happen for them in the end, but it certainly wasn't for want of sticking their necks out and giving it a go.

The Monday Club

It would probably be an exaggeration to say that without the drive, energy and wicked sense of anarchic playfulness that Nick Duckett brought to Reading in the late 70s the seismic upheavals that shook the UK music scene might have given the Borough a miss altogether. Yes, it's an exaggeration, but only just.

After his experiences with The Garage and Bones, Nick was convinced that the area's budding music scene had to be allowed to develop on its own terms and not on those of the people who were promoting at existing venues like The Target or even Cherry's Wine Bar. A musician himself, what Nick had in mind was rather more radical than any of the existing venues were likely to tolerate. He

READING CALLING. THE MONDAY CLUB.

Generally speaking, a more appropriate song of the Clashs to sum up the activity on the Reading scene would be "Reading's Burning (With Boredom Now)", but at least not everybody's sitting in a mire of lethargy and pessimism. Some cool dudes write this really cool fanzine (That's news to me - P.I.), and then there's the Monday Club. The Monday Club is a modest but highly commendable attempt to bring a few groups to Reading, and give a few local groups a chance to play. However, the venture suffers from a lamentable lack of support. If you live in or around Reading, and you want to know more about the Monday Club, then ring me - details elsewhere - or the clubs organiser Nick, on Reading 481637.

Eddie Snide's plea for support for The Monday Club

approached pubs and Church Halls across the town with the aim of encouraging local alternative-style music under the banner of, irony alert, The Monday Club, whilst ensuring that under no circumstances were they ever to stage any event on a Monday!

The Fox and Hounds in Caversham was one of the first to sign up, unknowingly accepting quite a challenge, its shiny Blue Plaque today commemorating Lennon and McCartney's brief tenure there as The Nerk Twins back in 1960 and not The Monday Club, sadly. These were often brief flirtations; landlords often being spooked by the anarchic nature of both the bands and the organisation. A brief spell in The Ship was terminated by the landlord who switched the power off mid performance by Monday Club stalwarts The Shrinking Men. They had a song called 'Twitching Fish' and used to get the audience to lay on their backs wriggling away like the aforementioned. The landlord exclaimed loudly that he wasn't having that sort of thing going on in his pub, or words to that effect.

Emmer Green Youth Club managed to prove rather more permanent a home for such fun and games, and a life saver for fourteen-year-old Stuart Osbourne, soon to be better known as Eddie Snide, his punk alter-ego, as getting in to see bands in pubs was obviously a problem. Now he could join in the fun. He remembers seeing Johnny and The Moondogs there, Denny and Dave Mills' youth club touring duo, who he describes as being "old-school rock and roll, but maaad!"

Steve Rolfe's crew, A Fast Crowd, were on the same bill and made quite an impression on the lad:

"They looked ordinary enough, but there was this guy kneeling on the floor howling something like, 'I am the last kid in the world!' and I identified with them right away."

Steve and A Fast Crowd had decided to throw in their lot with Nick's loose collective of talent, describing Nick as having a kind of Joe Meek approach to music, assembling a roster of stars and having band members interchangeable, part of a big team, Nick included. So, The Shrinking Men could go out as The Beevers and play a different set just by changing a couple of members. Maybe he could take this idea out on tour...

The Age of the Giant Quiffs

Those brave souls prepared to spend the time and risk their own money presenting live shows are, by definition, the lifeblood of the local music scene. Tony Long was a huge Buddy Holly fan who resolutely stuck to his guns when struck by the onslaught and energy of punk at the impressionable age of fifteen. He was glad he did, because within a year or two a strange mutant hybrid of punk and rockabilly began to emerge as the contemporary scene took a step backwards and embraced its rock and roll roots.

They called it psychobilly. Quiffs became huge toucan-like appendages, the crepe soles on the old blue suedes got thicker and thicker and the double basses got slapped faster and harder. Travelling up to London every weekend made Tony think he should be bringing all this good rocking back to his hometown. Teaming up with fellow fanatics Ged and Dizzy they booked King Kurt, a manic collection of improbable hairstyles, Elvis impersonations and Carry On-style humour for the very reasonable sum of £150, and secured Southcote-based SCAN PA hire along with legendary local soundman Grizz for the sonics. But would anybody turn up?

Answering a loud hammering on the door the lads were surprised to find a policeman enquiring when they were going to open to the public. Since gigs at The Caribbean Club rarely started before the pubs closed the policeman was concerned about what exactly the hundreds of people outside were going to do in the meantime. There were never any advance tickets sold, first come first served was the order of the day and this crowd was desperate not to miss out! It was the first of many, many successful evenings the boys promoted at The Caribbean Club, The Jive Dive, a burnt-out ex-snooker hall on the London Road they'd renamed, and The Majestic on the Caversham Road when their bookings warranted a larger capacity venue. Their promotions brought all the 80s alternative greats to the town including Alien Sex Fiend, The Stingrays, The Meteors, Red Lorry Yellow Lorry, The Membranes, Doctor and The Medics, Zodiac Mindwarp and the great Johnny Thunders of New York Dolls fame, among many, many others. What's more, locally based outfits on the verge of breaking through usually made up the bills and included The Coffin Nails, The Gathering, Diatribe, The Complaints and a host of others. Everyone was happy.

The Complaints   Johnny Thunders

Getting Johnny Thunders was a bit of a coup. The boys put him up in the somewhat less than five-star Tower House Hotel and secured local lads The Scanners as his backing band, just the way Chuck Berry operated on tour. So, on to the tiny Caribbean Club stage lurched Johnny with a syringe still poked into a vein. He fell over, got helped back up, someone plugged in his guitar and off he rocked. His was never going to be a long life though.

Security at the concerts the boys dealt with themselves, saying today:

"There might be a few scuffles, and you might have to eject the odd person, but that was all, which was surprising because of the liveliness of the music."

The Macholettes gig poster, 1983

Sadly, it didn't last, Tony noticing that some of the events were taking on a kind of football-style hooligan atmosphere. It culminated in windows being smashed and repeated attempts to set alight a bus carrying the fans of a Portsmouth-based band appearing one night, the two towns' football teams being deadly rivals in Division Two at that time. With no insurance cover and a sense that this sort of nonsense was only going to get worse the boys decided to call it a night. It had been a good run. Tony says today:

> "The timing was right for the type of scene that we brought to the town, but scenes change, and we all move on."

Fortunately, we can't move on without a mention of The Macholettes, the world's first boy band. Hmmm, maybe. There was certainly nobody else like them on the local scene, or anywhere else for that matter. Tony and fellow promoter Ged Athendriou were the core instigators of this inspired idea. Down their local they started making up synchronised dance routines to a couple of songs booming out of the jukebox, added Dizzy to the mix, rehearsed some more, and began to appear in pubs and clubs across the town. Initially, of course, it was just as a bit of a laugh, but they soon found themselves playing The Ace in Brixton, a venue that held around three thousand, with them squeezed in between King Kurt and The Pogues. They more than survived.

An easy act to present, they just plugged in the tape and off they went. Knowing a crowd of girls from the town who'd play ball with this playful conceit, when asked what they wanted as a rider when booked to play venues like the University they'd ask for twenty guest tickets. The girls would then all rush to the front, screaming and pulling at the boy's trousers in supposed feverish desire for these handsome be-quiffed hunks, the boy's sense of irony still just about intact.

Of course, their shelf life was brief, and they certainly didn't take themselves too seriously, even launching a competition to win a night out with the Macholette of your choice! Ah! The 80s! But they had worked up a routine that was surprisingly sharp, and funny with it.

6. The Bulmershe Connection

Berkshire College of Education

Always better known as Bulmershe College, Berkshire College of Education is today just another housing estate, the entire College site having been sold in 2011 and every building flattened. Its existence had been a precarious one after the merger with Reading University in 1989 and its subsequent loss of independent action.

For forty years it had provided a compact and intimate campus for fifteen hundred students, a high proportion of whom lived on site, giving the College a real community feel. In the late 70s it was still fulfilling the role for which it had been established, the training of teachers. The excellent facilities afforded to creative endeavour in art, drama, film studies and music gave the place the feel of an art school, a feeling that was strengthened with the entertainment bookings in the august hands of people like Geoff Benson, Rich Roberts, Chris Robinson and Pete Burton who turned Bridges Hall into an offshoot of the London pub and club scene in the late 70s. It is perhaps not surprising that the College threw up some rock and roll characters of its own during this period.

The Saga of Clayson and The Argonauts

Let's allow a couple of quotes from two who nailed their colours to Alan Clayson's mast in the late 70s set the scene. Here's Martin Lawrie, keyboard player:

> "Gigs with Alan were always unpredictable! We either got three encores or had to lock ourselves in the dressing room."

And this, from guitarist Mic Dover:

> "you never knew if the audience would want to hug you or beat you up."

Alan Clayson had, and still has, an unsettling effect on an audience, the delivery of his superbly crafted material coupled with the intensity of his on-stage persona being rarely seen in anyone functioning on the right side of sanity. Having painstakingly curated the band's mythology from its earliest incarnations he's remained an inspiration to very many of us who have followed his career over the last fifty years.

Launched at the College in the mid-70s, the Argonauts set sail upon graduation, gigged, toured relentlessly and got noticed. With songs informed by a mixture of the man's historical studies and his long-held love affair with British pop culture he was offering something that was very different lyrically, he and the band presenting it in a visually arresting way whilst positively delighting in making all those in attendance feel hot under the collar and uncomfortably close to the action. Early publicity photographs evoke memories of The Bonzo's, but by the late 70s during punk's incubation period there were few acts mining such a rich seam of eccentricity.

Picking up some serious press from intrigued journalists they were seized upon by Virgin Records eager to test the waters with a single and see where it might lead. For some reason, rather than choosing one of Clayson's own, a cover of a Wild Man Fisher do-wop parody, 'The Taster', was chosen, revealing Virgin's thinking as to the kind of artist they believed they had signed, the Wild Man being a protégé of Frank Zappa, and an eccentric street performer and diagnosed paranoid schizophrenic. The record's failure prompted the break-up of the band, Clayson finding the whole episode "damaging to both my confidence and credibility."

Of course, he bounced back, re-launching The Argonauts with a mostly fresh crew aided and abetted by Pete Cox, the man who had recognised and encouraged Tramp's talent prior to the formation of General Accident. They played Glastonbury in 1979 and released an LP in the 80s that finally revealed Clayson as the extraordinary songwriter and true original he'd been for the previous ten years. As did the release of an LP he produced and recorded with his hero, 60s hitmaker Dave Berry, an album which also included Berry singing four Clayson originals.

Still recording and performing, although mostly as a solo artist, he is of course internationally acknowledged as one of the finest and most prolific writers of music biographies working today, his catalogue including works on all four of The Beatles and a much-acclaimed account of the life of Jacques Brel. I suspect, however, that he'd exchange all his success as a writer for having just one of his songs make the Hit Parade. There's still time.

A Wraggle Taggle Gypsy

Damian Clarke's Damascene moment arrived in the guise of a performance by Showaddywaddy at Carlisle City Hall in the mid-70s. All flash and glamour, bright lights and gold lame suits, they seemed to have driven straight from the Top of the Pops studio at Television Centre and young Damian fell in love:

> "I'm a performer! I'm the sort of person who looks at the people on stage and just wants to be up there with them!"

Before arriving at Bulmershe in 1978, he'd been at Carlisle Art College, arriving one morning to find newspaper cuttings all over the studio depicting the previous evening's televisual bombshell, Bill Grundy losing by a knockout to The Sex Pistols.

> "My tutor had obviously been impressed because he'd started a punk band!"

Having been playing guitar from the age of eleven Damian was by now a good deal more than just a competent player but turned down his tutor's approach to join his band on a point of principle; he'd seen that some of the Sex Pistols' entourage had adorned themselves with swastikas and was less than impressed. He was, however, prepared to play a solo spot alongside his tutor's pet project at a forthcoming College function:

> "And there I was, dripping with sputum, playing these Chuck Berry rock and roll numbers, but really, really fast. The audience consisted of about a hundred people learning how to be punks for the night."

What Damian had very quickly discerned was that it was the hype, the outrage and the artifice that the media were buying into, whilst in fact it was the energy and freedom of expression that sold the scene to a generation's youth. For Damian, this was life changing:

> "Punk allowed me to be an individual."

Down South, Bullseye was to be the first and Spot The Dog the second band Damian formed in punk's wake, the latter releasing a single, Toy, that excited some record company interest. All about the rhythm, the complex, driving beats dominate both sides of an excellent piece of work. Angry, punky and political, is how Damian describes the band. Unfortunately, bass player Tim, brother of drummer Jonathan, headed off to drama college and that was that. Time for a rethink.

Curating nights of new, cutting-edge folk acts in the old Cap and Gown under the banner of The Pressgang Club brought people to the realisation that something very different was happening on the folk scene, and an evening in the club with the soon-to-be-very-famous American singer Michelle Shocked was a coup that turned into a local legend.

A chance meeting with one of his folk heroes, Maddy Prior, of Steeleye Span, resulted in the realisation that his two loves, folk music and punk, were not necessarily mutually exclusive. Catching a sell-out performance by The Pogues at The Hexagon merely confirmed this.

Bringing back drummer Jonathan into the fold and recording a version of 'The Wraggle Taggle Gypsies' sealed the deal. Pressgang, the band, came into being and swelled the ranks of what was now

Pressgang: George Whitfield, Iain 'Sprog' Aird, Jonathan Kirby and Damian Clarke

being referred to as the rogue folk movement, returning a sense of fun, urgency and relevance to folk-derived music. As in any other form of established musical tradition, there is a constantly evolving generational battle between the traditionalists and the new wave of modernisers and Pressgang's controversial stance may have been perceived as anti-folk by the traditionalists, but it was no more so than punk was anti-rock, and the negativity from the old-school folkies merely served to strengthen their identity.

With keyboard player George Whitfield, bassist Sprog and Jonathan Kirby on drums they recorded a much sought-after LP, turned professional, gigged and toured relentlessly both home and abroad for twenty years, then split up and reformed for another eight. And Damian is still going strong, performing and recording, writing and adapting and as determined as ever not to be a part of the folk mainstream. He much prefers to exist on the fringe where he can play, create, and, crucially, speak his mind freely without compromise. Now that's pure punk attitude for you.

And Here Come The Girls

The Stranglers had some great tunes but were never fully accepted as a punk band. They hired strippers for some stage shows. Not cool. The punk movement embraced true believers regardless of sex or sexual orientation in a way that was still some way off for the mainstream. Punk was an equal opportunities employer from the start, New Yorker Patti Smith living the life long before Malcolm McLaren even thought about creating his own pet monsters and delivering them to Vivienne Westwood to dress. But Siouxsie Sioux wasn't far behind, helping to make bondage and fetish clothing an integral part of the punk look whilst propelling a slew of singles and LPs into the charts. She played Bones Club, as did The Slits, formed after a chance encounter at a Patti Smith gig, and Penetration, fronted by the relentlessly intense Pauline Murray. The leather-jacketed Gaye Advert, bass player with The Adverts became an iconic figure on the scene until she tired of it, and then there was Poly Styrene, famous for her dental braces, Day-Glo outfits and mixed-race heritage. And for being as unconventional a singer in front of a band as it was possible to be.

Siouxsie Sioux, Patti Smith, Tina Weymouth, Pauline Murray

The Great Mistakes promo photo (with Jo Morris in front) anda 1981 gig poster

Fourteen-year-old Southlands' pupil Jo Morris found these women inspirational. She took up playing the bass after watching American art-punks Talking Heads:

"I watched Tina Weymouth like a hawk. She and Gaye Advert were the only female bassists I had ever seen apart from me! Today there are way more female musicians and that's a legacy of punk."

She was brought up in a household where pop music was banned by a father acting like a Victorian patriarch, her only connection with modern pop culture coming from watching *Top of the Pops* at a friend's house. She and her schoolmates were delighted by the Bill Grundy episode:

> "We were thirteen. It was like us versus authority, and we realised that we had allies."

Joining a music club at school opened her eyes to the breadth of material that came under the rock and pop banner. In an unconventional move her teacher, Clive Hacker, the man who had been booted off the stage by The Slits, asked her to join a band he was putting together. They would eventually become The Great Mistakes. Everybody she was mixing with on the scene was a lot older than her but says she was always treated with the utmost respect. Much to her surprise, her father did a one-eighty and came right on side with it all, driving her to gigs and watching his daughter's performances proudly from the wings. Animated and excited as she recounted her experiences with the band, she says she had the time of her life:

> "Punk was a unique happening that just gave everyone permission to get up and do something! I've always felt sorry for subsequent generations who missed out."

For Jo, playing bass for The Great Mistakes was quite obviously a life changing experience:

> "I'd gone from not really listening to music at all to almost drowning in this fantastic, brilliant scene full of these amazing people and I thought, this is where I belong, with all the misfits and eccentrics. I didn't know what I was looking for but here it was!"

The Bulmershe Band Factory

The first live band that Jimmy the Punk actually got in to see was Double Xposure at The Three Tuns on the Wokingham Road in early 1978. Elated that he'd gained access, being still under-age, he described the band as having a new wave feel about them, more art school rock than punk, but danceable. Inevitably, not being the type to just stand and clap politely, he was involved in an incident:

> "I remember these women trying to rip my trousers off! They took a fancy to my tight trousers. I had to take the safety pins off my coat and put my trousers back together!"

Double Xposure in photographic pun shock!

He was watching a troupe of ex-Bulmershe students led by guitarist Steve Gordon who'd followed Clayson's Argonauts out of Bulmershe and, like Clayson's crew, offered up a visual as well as a musical experience. For an up-coming appearance at The Merry Maidens they were being advertised in the local press as

"A seven-piece harmony group, with three attractive girls and four boys."

You'll have picked up that the venue hired a lot of cabaret-style acts, and if singer Alison Rolls' description of a song they performed called 'Chip City', named after a Bulmershe canteen's restricted offerings, is anything to go by they'd have fitted right in there:

"Annie [De Lima] and I, in matching skin-tight dresses split to the top of our thighs, would dance onto the stage holding aloft a giant burger made from foam. It was a highlight of the show!"

Their material was generally light-hearted and suitable for theatrical interpretation, their approach to the business best summed up by a single publicity photograph depicting the whole band sitting together fully dressed except for the double exposure of a pair of very naked buttocks!

With the break-up of the original Argonauts, guitarist Mic Dover was looking to start afresh with a new band, and since he was already pretty chummy with Alison, the couple later marrying, she jumped aboard and signed up: "it wasn't a complete surprise when Mic asked me and our drummer Steve Sawtell to leave Double Xposure and the frivolous frolicking around to form a new band. A serious one."

That band became Between Pictures and quickly picked up a very strong following as regulars at The Target, Cherry's and High Wycombe's Nags Head. Local fanzine *Grinding Halt* caught up with them playing that famous double-header with The Romantix at the Tech:

> "(They) are a band to keep an eye on.... And a trip to see them won't, I assure you, be a waste of time."

This was an early gig for them, their music fitting rather neatly into a post-punk, new wave sound, incorporating those pronounced

Between Pictures

reggae touches that were all the rage at the end of the decade. But achieving this necessitated ditching their original drummer, Steve. Alison explains:

> "The first time you have to sack a mate from a band you know that it has become something more than just a mess around."

A tough decision but evidently justified by the quality of the two singles the band released subsequently; the ever-relevant 'Treat Me Like An Equal', and the fabulously catchy 'Birthday Card', with its up-tempo ska feel, trailing echo and Joe Meek-style guitar tone. They both perfectly showcased a sound that should have brought those major labels knocking, with Alison out front, a star in the making, combining a mesmerising on-stage presence with a powerful, distinctive and original voice. A band on the up was the verdict of all those who saw them as they gigged their way across the town and the country, from London's Marquee Club to a Greenham Common Peace Rally and a Top Rank appearance with Killing Joke. A strange affair, that one, the Rank's management insisting that the paying public remove their boots before entry, having been alerted to a possible clash between punks and skins. The audience then consisted of hundreds of the aforementioned sliding around the dancefloor in their socks!

> "Our whole lives revolved around playing the next gig, the one that could launch our career… we were certainly having fun and have great memories of being part of a very vibrant live music scene in the late 70s and early 80s."

Unfortunately, the next gig failed to launch their career after all, and Alison and Mic sensed that the band had gone as far as it was likely to go. It was time for a reset and a rethink.

An ad placed in Melody Maker for a bass player brought forth Ali McMordie, formerly with punk legends Stiff Little Fingers and whose already-established London-based music business connections quickly paid dividends. The five-piece outfit, now consisting of Mic and Alison, McMordie, drummer John Reynolds, and Mike Clowes on keyboards, called themselves Friction Groove, and made their debut supporting the hitmaking British soul duo Imagination at the University.

The Festival Against The Missiles took place at Greenham Common on 20 April 1981, and at which acclaimed actress Julie Christie spoke.

Alison was at this time working with ace producer Martin Rushent at his Streatley studio, and it was a simple enough job to pass him a demo the band had recorded for his advice. He was impressed and helped them to re-record it with a view to making Mic and Alison a deal, minus the rest of the band. Ironically, as it turned out, they rejected his offer, but, generous to a fault, he allowed them to hang on to the result of their combined efforts. This recording of their song, 'Time Bomb', went on to secure a deal with the mighty Atlantic Records, home of the likes of Led Zeppelin and Aretha Franklin, and must have seemed like the best of all possible outcomes.

Sadly, it wasn't. An album, *The Black Box*, was recorded partly in Berlin where the band found themselves billeted in a hotel close to Checkpoint Charlie, the physical, psychological and ideological division of the city still solid as a rock in 84. Might be fun to take the van, (hired from Adrian's Van Hire in Winnersh, the go-to company used by every band in the region) across the border into the East for a bit of sightseeing, they thought. Ah, those sinister East German border guards: "You a rock group? Do you like Smokie?"

The record should have propelled the band into orbit, but just didn't, and the guy who had signed them to Atlantic quit the company, leaving them with little support in the boardroom. Mic knew that

Friction Groove looking particularly dapper

the label wouldn't really bother to promote the LP, and wasn't very happy at the way it had turned out anyway. Sinead O'Connor, who was in the process of recording her first album, poached Mike, Ali and John from The Groove to record with her. Mic turned down the offer and in so doing turned his back on a lifetime of royalties for the global smash hit, Nothing Compares 2 U! He seems philosophical enough about it now though:

> "you rock, you roll, then you hang up your plectrum and name drop into your beer to anyone who'll listen."

Anyone For Tea?

In January of 1984 a Reading band's video aired on the cult Friday evening show, The Tube, in an edition that also included the premieres of the Frankie Goes To Hollywood number 'Relax' and Queen's 'Radio Gaga', pretty auspicious company for the showing of a promo that cost a pittance to shoot and mostly starred ex-members of The K9s and Double Xposure. They called themselves The Geisha Girls, and the video was created to advertise their maddeningly catchy new single, 'I'm A Teapot'.

The three girl singers, Anne De Lima, Jill Myhill and Lez Hannibal had been flown up to Newcastle, interviewed live and asked how much this funny, crazy video had cost to make. Jools Holland's conversation with the studio audience then virtually followed the script of those maddening Wowcher commercials: which video do you prefer, studio? The one by Queen costing three hundred thousand, or the one by The Geisha Girls costing three hundred? The Geisha Girls video, apparently, hands down.

With a gig to do at Reading University the same evening the trio caught a seven thirty flight back to Heathrow and arrived at Bridges Hall in their stage gear and ready to rock:

> "This is a number you might already have heard this evening. I'm A Teapot!"

The packed hall erupted as the intro started, the band going on to play a blinder that night.

A consciously low-budget British take on The B-52's, the trio of girl singers looked and sounded a treat as they vocalised the boys'

Geisha Girls single I'm A Teapot

The Complaints' first single, There Were Rays Coming Out Of Their Eyes

amusing but generally pertinent attempts at writing feminist lyrics. Crucially, they also played catchy tunes you could dance to. Sprog, Greg and Kevin had brought the K9s' anarchic sense of fun to the party along with much of their fan base, and Mark Chapman and Anne, the Bulmershe connection here, a bit of art-school class. Crucially, Mark's skills as a budding film director, skills later utilised in setting up a successful video production company, were evident to all with this 'I'm A Teapot' three hundred quid blockbuster.

Undoubtedly, though, it was the trio of girl singers that got the band noticed. Lez wasn't known as Big Lez for nothing. She was a huge presence on and off stage and the possessor of a fine voice. Flanked by the diminutive figures of Jill and Anne, all in their matching costumes, the band looked set to go places, and it wasn't exactly a hindrance to have Lez working days as Sting's cleaner either. When Sprog was short of a bass guitar for a gig, and his guitar was a rather specialist number, she got Sting to send his own identical instrument over in a taxi, the man himself turning up at a Dingwalls' gig a few days later and chatting amicably with the band post-performance.

Opinions differ as to why Lez quit the band, but it eventually proved to be a fatal blow, the release of a second single, 'Slave of Love', having failed to build on the interest created by the first. Now calling themselves The Purple Turtles they proceeded to cash in on the fashionable return of psychedelia and, according to Sprog, would have been the ideal backing band for a certain Austin "Danger" Powers had he been around at the time. They created songs by placing short phrases in a hat and drawing them out to make nonsensical acid-tinged song titles. Far out man! And, of course, that name lives on in Reading...

The Caped Crusaders

When we in The Complaints finally found the right blend of musicians we became, for a couple of years in the mid-80s, the most popular band on the local circuit, our blend of ridiculously over-the-top theatrics, ninety-mile-an-hour delivery and daft but dark lyrics proving to be a winning formula. We were never regarded as a cool proposition though, despite our first single, 'There Were Rays Coming Out Of Their Eyes', becoming a John Peel favourite.

Why? Because there was nothing remotely fashionable or stylish about us. Unashamedly populist, our aim was simply to be at the epicentre of a good night out. The shows were often chaotic affairs and the fans boisterous, a combination which, like The K9s before us, too often resulted in venues striking the band off their list of upcoming attractions to avoid further trouble.

With Billy Seago on drums and Richard Jackman on guitar, both formerly with Theale Green School heavy rockers TNT, myself on beginner's bass guitar and vocals, the line-up was completed with Richard's partner and now wife of forty years Celia Reed on keyboards, my then girlfriend Julie gamely if reluctantly agreeing to mix the live sound. We must have played every pub between Reading and Southampton that booked live music, sometimes in tandem with our great friends in Blind Date, and too often to just a handful of bewildered customers in places I have never again been able to find on a map! Peasmarsh Social Club anyone? Something had to change.

So, to properly summon up the spirit and manic theatricals of ex-Reading University philosophy student Arthur Brown and the brittle genius of Syd Barrett-era Pink Floyd, Billy came out from behind his drums, and I handed the bass over to those who could actually play, initially Rob Kemp, then Nick Fish and finally Ian Munt, and quite suddenly we were worth the price of admission. With Billy and me now free to spread menace on stage with our white-painted faces and red hair our behaviour became increasingly unhinged, Billy becoming a mad, demonic Coati Mundi to my frighteningly, intensely, disturbed King Creole. Audiences were liberally splattered with Kensington Gore, porridge, chicken feathers, bananas or whatever one of us had picked up cheap for the night's entertainment, the highlight always being the unleashing of Billy to threaten and cajole those present and whip them into a frenzy. Out into the crowd he went, and always on the end of a rope, the easier to retrieve him if things turned rough! Unsurprisingly, a host of first-rate musicians came and went, Richard remaining to keep this horror show rockin'. It was intense, but it couldn't last, and we collapsed at the decade's end when for one of us the infernal torments acted out nightly became all too real for it to continue.

We certainly made a mark, it being noticeable just how many acts seemed to recognise the importance of presentation after sharing a stage with us. Others, scoffing at such crowd-pleasing antics, regarded us as little more than crass exhibitionists. But I was amazed when working in The Sound Machine just how many people seemed to remember us with genuine affection and wondered if there might just be a chance we'd do it all again one day…

And Finally For Something Completely Diferent

In a book whose subject matter is centred around the explosion of musical creativity in the Reading area after the screening of the Bill Grundy interview it might seem strange to include a band like Twelfth Night. Formed in the last years of the 70s at Reading University their music is about as far removed from the raucous minimalism associated with punk as it is possible to get. In fact, they seemed to be anxious to involve themselves in the sounds and image of a form of music that punks seemed most eager to distance themselves from: Prog. It wasn't just the music punks were rejecting either, but the sheer overblown pretentiousness of many of the music's exponents.

But Twelfth Night's drummer Brian Devoil had been around a bit. As a student he'd always put something together for the University's

Battle of the Bands competition and then tried his hand at managing the blossoming career of Clayson and The Argonauts, the Bulmershe connection here. When Clayson supported The Jam at the 100 Club drummer Rick Buckler borrowed a fiver from him which he never saw again. Early lesson in showbiz right there! A short time later he could be found laying down the beat for those Zinzan Street irregulars Trash as punk grabbed the nation by the throat.

Right from their early days Twelfth Night were selling home-made cassettes at gigs and via mail-order, the DIY philosophy of punk in action. And no, they were unlikely to attract many of The K9s' hardcore punk crew to The Target whilst playing lengthy instrumental stuff like 'Sequences', a recorded version of which takes up a whole side of the live album they recorded there.

Twelfth Night's Smiling At Grief was available on cassette at gigs and via mail-order

Let's face it, the singlemindedness that the band showed in putting their music out into a world that on the surface appeared almost universally hostile to them takes some doing. And that photograph on the back of The Target live LP from 1981, the one where every member of the band has long, luxuriant hair and wears flares and cheesecloth, the one that was shot in soft focus? Come on! That's a band saying, fuck you, we do this our way!

And they did. They got there before Marillion, spearheading the dawn of New Prog in the 80s, were the first Reading-based band to play the Festival, not once but twice, and with better luck it would have been three times, and they got signed by Virgin who subsequently released a series of seven and twelve inch singles, a picture disc and an extremely lavishly packaged LP.

I don't have the space here to document all the ups and downs of the band's career. They were a success by anybody's standards, but they should have been huge. Some notably less successful musicians on the local scene might have scoffed at all this retro prog "nonsense" but they all recognised a powerful and imaginative musical creation when they saw one. No way was Jo Morris a fan of theirs before seeing them at The Target, but she was "totally blown away" by the sheer scale and ambition of the music they created. Hats off to 'em.

Twelfth Night badge, Reading Festival 1983

7. Working For You

The Soundman Keeps His in the Toilet

You quickly discover that you need a range of people working on your behalf to ensure that your appearances are as smooth-running and trouble-free as possible, and by the end of the 70s sound technology had developed to the point where an increasing amount of complex, highly technical equipment was required. With all hands to the pumps there was no problem getting the gear into the venue and setting it all up, but you needed somebody out front to make sense of it all, somebody like Grizz, or this fellow, Chris Trimby.

Going to see The Jam at The Top Rank had been a game-changer for the apprentice printer and so, dressed in the appropriate punk clothing, he became a regular face in Bones, Cherry's and The Star and fell for the illusion of all that social turmoil the music seemed to be promising. He began to think that there might just be more to life than overseeing the printing of a never-ending stream of red Oxo Cube boxes for months on end.

A big fan of Between Pictures, he was asked if he'd like to try out as their sound engineer, mixing the out-front sound through the band's own PA system. It turned out that Chris had found his calling in life, and he gained a wealth of experience when he threw in his lot with Scan PA Hire, based in a garage in Southcote, the go-to business for all local bands when a bigger rig was required for venues like The Majestic.

Ex-Bulmershe social secretary Geoff Benson was aware of Chris' work with Between Pictures and was now employed as the lighting manager for the Marquee Organisation's in-house sound and light company ENTEC, and recommended the ambitious youngster to the company. Chris was finally able to quit the print business and start work as a full-time sound engineer with ENTEC, based at Shepperton Studios.

He quickly discovered that there was more to the business than just travelling up and down the motorway system setting up in a different town every night, mixing the sound and then heading off to the next stop on a tour. So, he took the option to become the live sound and monitor mixer on Channel 4's music magazine show, *The*

Tube and found himself travelling up to the same town, Newcastle, every Friday for the duration of a series. Doing TV obviously suited him because he later did four years on *TFI Friday* and six on *Top of The Pops*, and gradually a pattern emerged as he prioritised TV work over the winter months and festivals throughout the summer.

Still touring and sound mixing for some of the biggest names in the business, there really can't be many Reading residents who've been the recipients of an Emmy Award, can there? Chris was involved with an American show called *Tribute to Heroes*, a phone-in event to raise money in the wake of 9/11 for the firemen and emergency services personnel impacted by that terrible event. The British segment was filmed in the *Top of the Pops* studio and featured Sting and U2. Chris mixed the sound for the TV feed. If you happen to pop round for a cuppa it's proudly displayed in his downstairs loo!

Barry The Fence

Local commercial radio station, Radio 210, began broadcasting in March 1976, initially transmitting from a mast atop The Butts Centre and offering what might seem today to be an enticingly eclectic mix of musical programming, especially from 7pm onwards. Country, jazz, reggae and folk music, often recorded live from local clubs and venues, all had their own dedicated programs.

Weekends featured a Rock Show, a Soul Show, and one curiously titled *Off The Wall*, presented by a young DJ by the name of Jonathan Richards who played music of a slightly left-field, independent nature. Concert promoter and budding broadcaster Barry O'Brien had contacted the show hoping for some on-air publicity for an event he was hosting and the two hit it off immediately, with Jonathan suggesting Barry might like to sort through the box-loads of tapes he had received from local musicians with the aim of including a selection on the show. The result was that this hour-long broadcast rapidly became a must-listen for musicians and gig goers across the Thames Valley, with Barry, now known simply as The Fence to avoid personal hassles from over-eager contributors, presenting alongside Jonathan.

Singles, flexi discs and tapes sent in from across the Valley featured, as did interviews with local musicians, reviews of shows by invited guests, gig guides, live studio sessions and even outside broadcasts.

One of Barry The Fence's compilation cassettes in aid of his chosen charities, Give A Child A Chance and Dellwood Cancer Appeal.

Records were reviewed and local musical gossip discussed in an entertaining, fun-packed hour, and a regular fanzine reflecting the show's content rapidly became another platform for listener's contributions.

In fact, the entire show was really an audio fanzine, everything tumbled together and held in place by the slick professionalism of Jonathan Richards, with the marshalling of the mountains of quality material sent in by the ever-enthusiastic listeners introduced by The Fence himself. Charity gigs were organised, usually featuring artists frequently heard on the show and which, alongside the release of compilation cassettes and a very collectable LP, provided some cash for Barry's favoured charity, Give A Child A Chance.

I was a guest in the packed studio one Christmas to witness a live performance by Mike Cooper and Terry Clarke and acted as an interviewer for an outside broadcast live from Bracknell's Cellar Bar the following yule. It was an hour of broadcasting that sparked with spontaneity, and as a platform for the talent emerging from the local scene through the 80s it couldn't have been bettered. Always lively, contributors were only asked to refrain from swearing and to avoid criticism of the advertisers, this being commercial radio, everything else was fair game. It was too good to last; the business was sold towards the end of the 80s and the new owners wanted a more mainstream format introduced across the station. Of course they did.

Fanzines

You have a band. Getting written about is almost as good as hearing your music on the radio. Being the featured artists in a full-page spread in a national music weekly like *Melody Maker*, as Clayson and the Argonauts were in early 1977, or at least having your gigs and singles reviewed in the nationals like Trash a little later might well have been your aim. To start with, you settled for a piece in your local press where the writing tended to follow the template of a press release, all gushing optimism topped with a generous sprinkling of wishful thinking. It's all publicity though and gets your name out there.

Fanzines were different. They may not have been an invention of the punk explosion, but they rapidly proliferated in the face of the established press's hostility. Sometimes typed, sometimes handwritten, sometimes photocopied, sometimes spirit duplicated, there might only be twenty copies of an issue ever produced, stapled and sold for a few pence at a K9s gig, but they existed because their creator loved the scene so much they just had to get involved.

The first locally produced 'zine to hit the streets of Reading came in early 1978 and laid down its challenge: *Kiss This*. Created by the estimable team of Rolfe, Pope, Kelly and Williams, it should today be viewed as a valuable historical document, perfectly capturing as it does a special moment in the history of the Borough by communicating a breathless excitement with all things punk, much of it Bones Club-related.

Kiss This fanzine

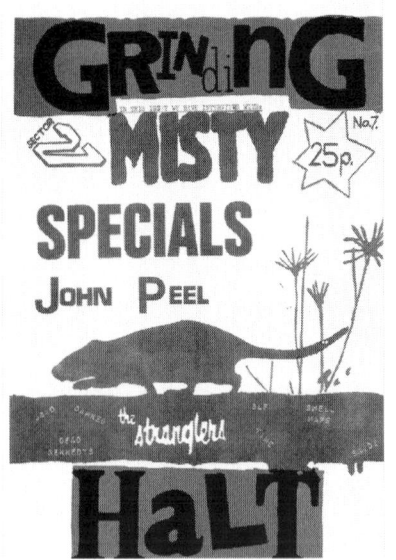
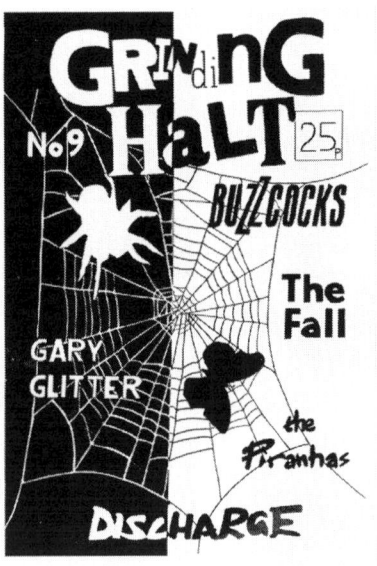

Grinding Halt covers: issue nos. 3, 5, 7 and 9

Perhaps too wrapped up in their own musical adventures to bother with a second edition the baton was eventually taken up by Oratory School pupil Stuart Osbourne, aka Eddie Snide and his school mates Captain Callous and Pig Ignorant, joke names they'd given each other before they started their fanzine, Eddie being only fourteen years old after all.

They called their creation *Grinding Halt*, after a song by The Cure, and between 1979 and 1981 produced twelve issues. It became one of the most popular titles in the UK with as many as two and a half thousand copies being created for national distribution, by Rough Trade among others, local fans being able to get copies at Quicksilver Records.

It's an excellent read, and the amount of care, attention and love that went into each issue is everywhere apparent. Virtually every notable act that could even be vaguely termed punk or post punk was tracked down and interviewed, from The Cure and The Damned to John Peel and The Specials, the latter after their TV appearance with our own General Accident, Eddie Snide a visible presence in the audience there. The only time their trusty tape recorder failed to work just had to be the time when they were the UK's only fanzine to be granted an interview with The Ramones on their 1980 UK tour, Joey Ramone blagging a pen off a reluctant bystander so the boys could take notes.

Singles and LPs were reviewed, readers' polls were published, cartoons drawn, and gigs reviewed, and not just local ones. The covers for each edition are eye-catching and imaginative, the one for issue no. 7 anticipating Banksy by twenty-odd years. And local bands were everywhere championed, reviewed and supported; a big deal as, of course, the magazine was nationally distributed. The publication is today held in great esteem and regarded as one of the very best in the genre. And rightly so.

There were others, and *Exposure* and *Utterance* were probably the best of them, and fair play to the latter for trying to sell the idea of something they called the Thamesbeat Phenomenon. Premature, possibly, but they were proved to be spot-on by the decade's end.

Both 'zines are heavy on local band coverage, reviewing gigs, singles and tapes sent to the Woodley and Whitley addresses provided. Interviews with local talent like The Ballistics and Diatribe

Exposure and *Utterance* fanzines

are informative without being exhaustingly dense, and they helped to bring to the town's attention up-and-coming outfits like the glorious but short-lived trio Instant Fish, the almost numberless legions of the all-action Ant Hill Mob, and the gloomy but magnificent Gathering among almost countless others. They did a fine job for as long as they lasted, and in *Utterance's* case for a good chunk of the 80s as editions ran well into the teens. Perfectly documenting the excitement and frantic creativity bursting out across the town, they wore their politics on their sleeve, voiced honest opinions and were never smug or condescending. Reading them today is like opening a treasured photo album where the sun shines in every snap, on every day, forever.

8. A Dummy's Guide to Setting Up Your Own Record Label

Flexi Discs and The Dog's Breath

The chances of getting signed up by a record company were always slim, so why bother waiting? Manchester's Buzzcocks had led the way by forming their own record label and releasing the EP Spiral Scratch in January of 1977. By all clubbing together you could afford to do this, but there was a cheaper alternative: the flexi disc.

Releasing a flexi got you noticed, although they were not really a step-up in sound quality from the cassette, or of longevity, being easily rendered unplayable by becoming creased. The grooves were usually just cut on one side, but in all other respects this was a seven-inch single, it just wouldn't stack on the old Dansette. With a paper cover and a plastic envelope, though, it looked just like the real thing. They made an impressive offering for fans and kinda hinted you were going places.

Often included as giveaways in the national music press, the boys at *Grinding Halt* thought they'd try the idea out with their twelfth issue. Having been promoting concerts to raise money for the magazine, it seemed like the logical next step to set up a record label. They approached The K9s who offered a couple of tracks but which, after some delay, were rejected by the French company pressing the disc either due to the obscene nature of the material, or for copyright reasons. The boys, true to form, had changed the words to the Shangri-La's 'Leader of the Pack' to the subversively puerile Dose of the Clap! Fearful of losing their hefty deposit, Eddie Snide stepped in and substituted the two tracks he had recorded with Sub Active, and the pressing went ahead. The unresolved issue of the band's instrument tunings at Audiogenic were therefore made available to anyone who bought Issue 12 and has left Eddie trying to cover for it ever since.

A year earlier, K9s bass-player Sprog had taken the decision to set up a record company, Dog Breath Records, to release material by the band, and it turned out to be a lengthy and convoluted process. He ended up joining The Mechanical Copyright Protection Society

Dog Breath Records logo, and the cover of the compilation album Too Loud To Scream

and The Musician's Union, then had to find a royalty accounting and processing business, an electro-plating business, and a pressing plant, in this case Ice Records in London, run by Eddie Grant's dad. Eventually, it was a case of everybody coming round to his house to stick the labels on the records. A distributor agreed to do what distributors do and the record sold well, however nobody has any recollection of ever receiving any money for all their hard work. Oh well. Dog Breath Records went on to release singles by The Geisha Girls and The Complaints, and the compilation album *Too Loud To Scream* before curling up for a long sleep.

Pop Records, the Record Label

Nick Duckett ran a record label and a shop using the same name, just like, er, Richard Branson! Called Pop Records, the label's first seven-inch single was released in 1980 and featured a design that looked awfully familiar. Why so? Because being faithful once again to the confrontational nature of punk, Nick had stolen the design from Top Rank International, the instantly recognisable red and white label depicting a hunky muscleman banging his gong. It was a risky move. Nick takes up the story:

"(They) took me to court, and I had a huge pile of papers from them several inches thick. They were after thousands of pounds... I had to move house several times to keep one step ahead of them. They actually sent private detectives after me!"

Their lawyers finally settled for a few hundred quid and for a disclaimer to be stuck to every copy of their third release, an EP shared between The Shrinking Men and The Beevers, two different bands but with almost the same personnel. A young Eddie Snide remembers turning up to one of Nick's Monday Club gigs and being allowed free entry if he spent an hour sticking gold labels over the rogue imprint. It stated:

"This record has no connection with the Top Rank Organisation, and Pop Records apologises for any confusion arising from the use of the 'man with gong' logo."

For Eddie, this was the way that punk should be, properly subversive.

Sadly, this was Pop Records final release due to some seriously bad luck. An enthusiastic distributor had taken all one thousand copies of their first release, the EP *Magnifico*, by El Seven and, buoyed up by the prospect of having at least a minor hit on his hands, Nick had another thousand pressed. As the band's second single was by now ready to go he had two thousand of that manufactured and dispatched to the distributor who then promptly went bust. Nick reckons that only a couple of hundred were ever sold.

He'd had the idea of promoting the first single by organising a Pop Records tour, initially featuring El Seven, Shrinking Men and the manic rockabilly of Johnny and The Moondogs. Advertised both locally and nationally the tour criss-crossed the South through the early months of 1981. So, how did it go, Nick?

"It was a complete and utter fiasco. It was madness really, sending three unknown bands to play venues up and down the country. One landlord... said they were the worst bands he'd ever seen."

Undaunted as ever, Nick decided to plough his energies into yet another venture: Pop Records, the shop.

The Last of the Independents? Not Quite

You headed east from Reading town centre and down The King's Road to find Pop Records, the shop, the first used-record store in town that organised their stock, as opposed to just tumbling it into crates and charging a pound fifty for each platter you salvaged. The shop also sold tickets to gigs, and the only place in town selling them for University promotions; social secretaries like Jez Dyer believing that the establishment attracted a better class of music lover and so was less likely to be selling tickets to riff-raff and troublemakers!

It was an excellent place to browse through recent stock arrivals, advertise for a drummer for your band, or perhaps even bump into one there. Sadly, Nick put the shutters up after a six-year run, unable to shake off a particularly persistent arm of The State but has compensated by organising record fairs across the South ever since.

Situated at the top of the escalator in The Butts Centre, throughout the late 70s and early 80s Quicksilver was probably the most important retailer of brand-new recorded music this side of Slough and London. They sold soul, dance, punk and metal, and crucially, products by local bands: singles, flexis, badges and fanzines. And reggae. Reggae was big business; they would stock a lot of Jamaican imports. Future record label boss John Blaney worked there from the late 70s and remembers his Saturdays spent behind the singles counter as being completely manic:

> "On a good day the crowd would be three deep. We could sell fifty copies of a single by an outfit like Crass, a band that never even remotely troubled the Top 20".

It was another great place to meet up and talk music as the staff were fans and musicians themselves. And it was also a Chart Return business, meaning that its sales were used to compile the national singles and albums charts for the week, including those used by the BBC. Since all the record company reps were aware of this, they would ply the staff with gifts to encourage them to, let's say, get a bit creative with the figures. This could all get a bit out of hand, apparently, but tended to balance out in the long run as you couldn't mask a record's lack of sales indefinitely.

At its zenith, the business ran three shops and a couple of in-store franchises. They promoted shows at the Top Rank with the likes of

Pop Records shop poster

Slade, Killing Joke, Bauhaus and The Stranglers. An up-and-coming Spandau Ballet cancelled their Reading Top Rank appearance having played Cardiff's the previous night vowing never to play another! Refunds, like most transactions at that time, were in cash, and John remembers going to the bank and collecting around two grand in one pound notes for the purpose and having to hide the loot inside his coat to get it back safely.

Scorpio live on stage – their single, Taking England by Storm, is a NWBHM classic

They too established their own label, Quicksilver Records, first mentioned in an article in *The Evening Post* in June 1977, touting Scorpio as their first signing and were, apparently, looking to sign other local acts. A gig at year's end in the recently opened Hexagon featuring them with Straight Shooter and The Tamica Band and advertised as a Quicksilver promo, suggested they had found some. But it was another three years before anything appeared on the label, and then it all proved to be a fleetingly short experiment, creating only four releases before being mothballed. There is quality in what they left behind, though. Scorpio's 'Taking England By Storm', and Predatür's 'Seen You Here' b/w 'Take A Walk' are both glorious additions to the NWBHM canon, and General Accident's 'Computer Dating' lives on as a neat reminder of a band transitioning from its raw punk origins and embracing something altogether more commercial.

Criminal Damage

In the numerous books that he has written over the last few years Chris Green comes across as a forthright and uncompromising individual, each entertaining volume focusing on a different aspect of his lifetime's obsession:

"Music is everything to me and has consumed my life like nothing else. It's the first thing I think about in the morning and the last thing I think about at night."

A punk six months prior to the Grundy incident, he formed his own band, The Kaotix, and then examined his options:

> "I had always dreamed of a career in pop music without ever really knowing what I was dreaming about or having the faintest idea of how to achieve it."

Not, as it turned out, as a musician, but as the boss of his own label. He started with a cassette imprint called X Cassettes and released music from two excellent local combos The Stills and Dig Dig Dig. He then fixed up a deal with London-based Illuminated Records for a compilation LP of Reading bands, many of them associated with Nick Duckett's Monday Club promotions. Offered the opportunity by Illuminated to set up his own label peddling something called UK Hardcore, (punk's 1980s incarnation, fast and aggressive), he teamed up with Yaron Levy of The Stills and grabbed at the opportunity, never really intending to release anything remotely along those lines but thinking it best to choose a suitably aggressive name for the label, Criminal Damage, to disguise the fact. Here was an opportunity tailor-made for him to do what he wanted to do the way he wanted to do it.

With the operation located in a tiny room in Fulham the label gravitated more towards the goth end of the market, creating a series of singles, EP's and the occasional LP by a host of the world's talented hopefuls, including their most successful long-term signing, The Membranes.

Financially, though, they were soon up against it, and Chris decided on a new start, relocating to Reading's Swansea Road and taking on a new partner, Ged Athendriou, co-promoter with fellow psychobilly fan Tony Long at The Paradise and Jive Dive. This time the label came together around a nucleus of Reading bands who had relocated to the Big City to be closer to the action, among them MB Hi-Power, Them Howlin' Horrors, The Jack Rubies and The Heart Throbs, showcase gigs being organised at The Paradise and the Majestic to provide funds for the label:

> "The summer of 86 proved to be an unforgettable highlight... Criminal Damage found a new identity far removed from the goth and ugly noise undercurrents of the past."

The new roster attracted some serious press interest but, sadly, didn't translate into sales, the label rapidly ceasing to be a viable financial concern and getting wound up in December of that year.

For all his dedication to the cause, Chris never ceased to be a punk at heart. Attracted to those musicians who were utterly determined to plough their own furrow, he set up the label and signed artists because he loved their music and wanted the rest of the world to hear them. Criminal Damage was responsible for the release of over sixty records, but today Chris is somewhat dismissive of it all:

> "Our groups released a few records, got a bit of attention for five minutes if they were lucky, and then disappeared."

It's bigger than that. They took to the stage, made their point and left, which is pure punk. Without the likes of Criminal Damage much of this music would not now exist, and you wouldn't get to hear just how much fun we were having back then. And since Cherry Red Records recently bought the entire back catalogue from our man you can now access it all through Spotify, so, don't just sit there, go fill your boots!

Criminal Damage Records logo

Compilation Albums

A relatively cheap way of preserving your band's musical talents for posterity was to get a track included on a compilation tape or LP, and several appeared throughout the 80s that featured singers and bands from the Thames Valley. Inclusion undoubtedly enhanced your profile.

Beyond The River. (An Open Door Stereo 33)
Illuminated Records OD 001 1982

This marked the start of Chris Green's relationship with the company that would enable him to set up Criminal Damage. A hard man to please, Chris was never happy with the result:

> "overall the album was as disappointing as all the other compilations being released around the same time, documenting similar local scenes."

Perhaps it would have been better as a live album, recorded at Emmer Green Youth Club, now that really would be a historically interesting document, but it ain't bad at all. El Seven contributed a decent pop song, as did John Townsend's other band, Movita. The Ballistics also stand out, commitment and integrity ingrained within their minimalist dub reggae vibe. Gang of Four have certainly influenced other offerings here, and The Shrinking Men sound as if they were having a ball.

Blast....From The Hip To The Heart.
Criminal Damage CR1 LP 140 1986

Chris is certainly more effusive about this one, still claiming to be extremely proud of it:

> "a cheap sampler of eleven groups and tracks showcasing my closest allies and friends during the last year of the label."

Although now based in Reading, the label drew talent from far and wide, but this album also features many former Reading-based individuals and combos, and it gets off to a cracking start with MB

Hi-Power, formerly simply The Ballistics, and their inventive slab of melodica-led dub. Other stand-out tracks come from those joyous-sounding scallywags, Them Howlin' Horrors, and a total gem from the stars of the near future, The Heart Throbs. At £2.99, this was money well spent.

8/10

Too Loud To Scream.
Dog Breath Records WOOF 12. 1985

Put together by Danny, Greg and Sprog of the Geisha Girls, many of the acts also featured in a series of promotional videos shot by another Geisha, Mark Chapman, for his video production business. The final product, the misspelt compilation *Local Heros*, was the perfect showcase for the directorial talents he'd demonstrated with The Geisha's nationally broadcast 'I'm A Teapot' promo.

For the LP, contributors were asked to stump up fifty quid. Danny remembers that they squeezed on as many tracks as possible to make it self-financing. It's fun, but patchy. Shooting The Rapids get things off to a good start, and there are some classy moments from Joker, Sideways Laughing and The Gathering, among others, and the contribution from the female trio, Likely Lads, is great fun.

6/10

The Final Tease.
Final Records FINAL LP 42 1987

Based in Woodley and set up and run by Tim Greaves, Final Records put this together in 87 and it showcases the gothier elements at large in the Thames Valley, with echoes of The Alarm, U2 and The Cult written all over most, but not all, of the material. No criticism this, as it merely reflected the pixie-booted times it was recorded in. Standards, however, are high, and this is well worth checking out.

7/10

Beyond The Fence Begins The Sky.
Plastic Head Records. PLAS LP 008 1987
Assembled by Barry O'Brien, one half of the Radio 210 team presenting *Off The Wall*, specifically to raise money for charity. With thirteen tracks in all, the album's stand-out songs open each side: Beat and The Devil side one and The Jeremiahs side two, but there are no weak tracks. As a reflection of radio-friendly indie-pop from the late 80s this collection would be hard to beat.

The Fence. A Charity Cassette in aid of Give a Child a Chance, and The Dellwood Cancer Appeal.
Tracksuit Tapes 1989

> "No-one who contributed to this tape in any way will be a penny better off as a result."

So says the legend on the insert. Full of quality stuff from the Thames Valley, including the excellent Home and Abroad, the U2-inspired Blood Oranges and live sensations Jo Jo Namoza and Pressgang. The tape exists as a reminder of when local radio was bold and happy to be the home of slightly anarchic programming. *Off The Wall* was a joyous part of that and much mourned. The tape carries a dedication:

> "In memory of *Off The Wall* – less a programme, more an attitude."

There were plenty of other tape compilations, but few have weathered the intervening years as well as vinyl, tending to unravel in your car stereo as all tapes eventually did. Reading's local listings magazine, *Red Rag*, compiled a list of a few of them, one described as being, "15 Hot Hits from Local Bands. 60 minutes for £3". Sounds like a bargain, especially as it included tracks by The Soft Dogs, The Lost Boys and Beating Time. You might have a copy stashed away in your attic. If so, give me a call...

9. Appearing in Town Tonite!

The Seize

By the early 80s the music had changed dramatically, the momentum of change partly fuelled by the affordability of the latest technology arriving from the Far East. As wide a variety of musical styles as had ever existed before were to be heard live on the local circuit. It seemed that everybody under the age of twenty-five wanted to play in a band, either directly because of, or as a reaction against, punk. The Seize were very much in the former category.

Had the band appeared at the tail-end of 1976 their records would today appear on every collection of songs purporting to represent the finest that the genre had to offer. But they were late starters and didn't really get under way until the latter part of 1979 when punk was rapidly mutating.

Formed by the brothers Newton, their material was bedroom spawned, Colin's nasal tones and pounding, primitive bass lines being driven relentlessly forward by his brother Chewy bashing the hell out of a series of boxes and biscuit tins, together distilling a sound that was the pure essence of punk in its original form. They teamed up with another pair of brothers, guitarists, Andy and Julian Stafford, and The Seize were born.

Summer of 1980 saw them all set to rock, their first appearance being as support in a Nick Duckett promotion at The Britannia Tap, a pub so tiny that the band literally stood nose to nose with its audience. Colin considered the evening a success on the grounds that they didn't get beaten up! A second gig at the Wokingham Rock Club with the same band, The Suspects, convinced them it was time to make a record. Audiogenic was booked, two tracks recorded, and their own label established: Why Not? Records.

All the parts arrived just before Christmas, the printed labels needing to be stuck to the records, the records inserted into covers. It was fortunate that John Peel's Roadshow was appearing at the University early in the New Year and the DJ was duly handed a copy, along with an amusing letter detailing the genesis of both the band and the record, 'Why?' b/w 'Grovelands Road'. He not only played it on his Radio 1 show but read out the letter as well. As a result, two distributors, Rough Trade and Small Wonder took a chance and

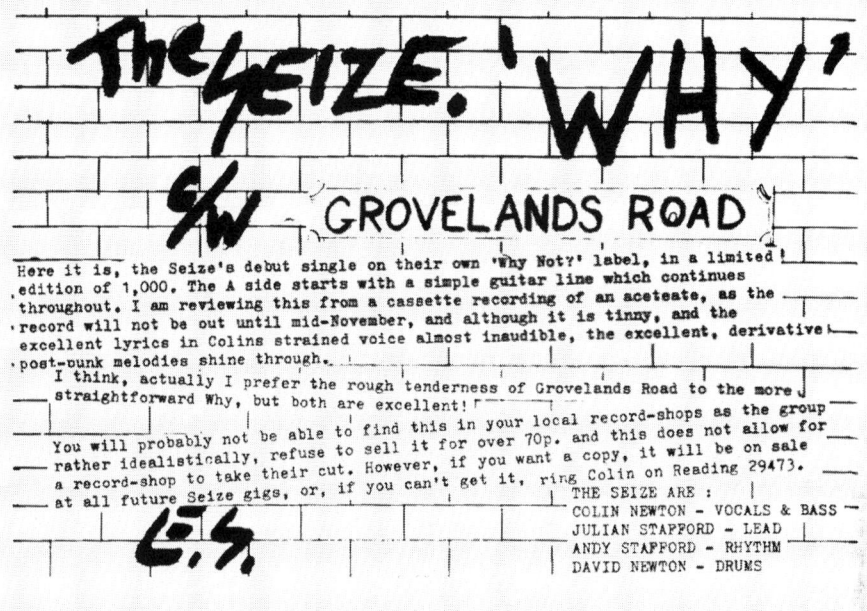

The Seize's debut single reviewed in *Grinding Halt*

placed their orders, rapid sales necessitating a second pressing. Both tracks rock along in their primitive, angst-filled way to destination punk in the simplest and most effective manner, making the sceptical believe that perhaps anyone could do this. But they didn't, and The Seize did.

Live appearances were occasional affairs. Two benefit appearances were made helping to raise funds for *Grinding Halt*, the first held in the University's Student Union and the second at the Hermann Gollancz Hall. This second one was an utter disaster, although no blame can be attached to either the fanzine or the bands who appeared that night. Some pathetic creatures took it upon themselves to scrawl swastikas on the walls of a building dedicated to the first British rabbi granted a knighthood. The offence caused by this jaw-dropping act of ignorance and stupidity beggars belief, even forty years later.

They played the second Nick Duckett-organised Alternative Reading Festival at Brock Barracks in the summer of 1981, Colin regarding this as their most accomplished performance, although with so few appearances to keep up the momentum the line-up of the band inevitably changed, but with the Newton brothers always retaining control. And more records followed. Their second release, the *Everybody Dies* EP, shows a marked improvement in sound quality from the first and came wrapped in a cover that might just have induced nightmares in sensitive souls. Their third, draped in the famous drawing of Jimmy Yoder Dancing Like A Dervish, and for which Clive Hacker of The Great Mistakes had been roped in to lend a hand on guitar, continued the run of form.

A prolonged period of inactivity saw the release of a mini-LP at the end of the decade for which Sprog and the ex-Quicksilver employee John Blaney had been recruited but by then they sounded like a markedly different proposition, poppy even, in places, and the brothers called a halt to the business soon afterwards. It had been fun, although Chewy admits that some of the gigs had been like playing in a war zone.

The musicianship of The Seize may have been basic, but it was sufficient to deliver exactly what was needed, smart lyrics, catchy hooks, incessant grinding rhythms and lyrical references to local characters and geography. The records change hands for big money today and the Newton brothers are rightly proud to have had the songs they thrashed out in their bedrooms pressed up on vinyl and played on national radio. And so they should be.

Predatür

No, Predatür were not a punk band. One look at Baz on stage, stripped to the waist, head thrown back and hair hanging down to his bum would show you that. The New Wave of British Heavy Metal banner was dreamt up by the music press to include those new rock acts who had been enthused by punk's energy and had applied it to heavy metal. Baz loved Status Quo, so he nicked the rhythms and stripped the sound back to its early 70s roots. It now fizzed with punk energy, audiences in the always-packed Target jumping for joy:

> "We were popular to the point that you couldn't get in. People were stacked up the stairs."

Quicksilver released their single, 'Take A Walk', in 1982, recorded at Matinee, and their man Kevin Heaton got the band involved with some of the company's promotions at the Top Rank, in both Cardiff and Reading, the Welsh booking as support to the much-fancied Persian Risk, the Reading appearance with the revitalised and born-again Slade, this one as a replacement for a support act stuck in the snow. Digging their very distinctive purple gig-rig out of the mountainous drifts, Predatür rode to the rescue.

Reflecting the band's rising profile, they were offered a Saturday afternoon slot at the 1983 Festival, headliners that day being the metal behemoth that was Black Sabbath, Purley resident Ian Gillan on vocals at this time. Unfortunately, rearrangements saw the boys pushed into doing the less prestigious opening slot on the Friday and they were persuaded by Kevin to drop it. As compensation, he included them in the Bank Holiday spectacular three days later that Quicksilver had organised at the Top Rank to take advantage of all the Festival fans still in town. Headlined by rising stars Tygers of Pan Tang and Praying Mantis, the capacity crowd saw the local boys blow the roof off.

The big time never materialised for Predatür in the end, but after a lucrative spell playing guitar with ex-Status Quo drummer John Coghlan's band Diesel they lived again, recently releasing an album, *Weidenhaus*, that does an awful lot more than just secure their legacy. There has always been an infectious honesty and lack of pretension about the band. They looked like they were having fun, loved what they did and seemed completely unconcerned about what the world thought of them. Actually, the world thought they were great, and still does, with gigs still being planned as I write.

In fact, the town was awash with first class rock and metal acts during this period. Steve Cresswell's outfit Scorpio's single, 'Taking England by Storm', offers up some punk-like simplicity, its lack of flash, grinding guitar riff and vocal hollerings reminiscent of Saxon's 'Wheels of Steel' but with a keyboard solo rather than the expected piece of guitar shredding.

Featuring ex-Predatür guitarist John Benham, Dog'ouse also came out of Woodcote and featured ex-Ten Years After keyboard player Chich Churchill, the guy who had lent Predatür all that equipment. They accepted an invitation to open Friday's proceedings at the 1986 Festival, were more than warmly received and were then followed on stage by a man who had become a fixture at The Target for many years, the much-loved Larry Miller and his Band. With possibly the finest rhythm section available locally, Simon Baker on drums and Andy Allen on bass, they had recorded their first LP at Matinee back in 1982. *Right Chaps!* included a tribute to his great mate from Predatür, Baz, and as the whole LP motors along with a kind of Quo-inspired punkiness, he'd obviously been quite an influence. It's raw and it's fun, but it would be fourteen years before he recorded another, and then they came thick and fast until a stroke in 2015 brought his international career to a halt. He'd been recording his next LP when he was struck down, but thankfully, he eventually recovered enough to finish the job he'd started.

There just isn't the space here to give credit to all the excellent rock bands that emerged in the town. Deserving of a book of their own I should mention here the likes of Turbo, Hazzard, Special Brew, Iron Heart, White Speed, and The Tamiko Band, fronted by the Roberts sisters Teri and Tami in perfect vocal harmony. The Roger Barnes-fronted Motley Crew were more of an R'n'B band but seemed to be on an almost endless loop of appearances from the mid-70s onwards. They came over like a cross between Dr Feelgood and Graham Parker and left behind an excellent single, 'City Girl', appropriately enough on the Cherry's label, that Wine Bar being a regular haunt for them, before morphing into the seemingly immortal Jive Alive, and passing the Borough's blues baton to the boys of the excellent Blues Cruise.

Three Amigos:
Steve Rolfe, Gary Jones and John Townsend

In the early 80s Steve Rolfe had a bet with a mate to see who could play with the most bands over the course of a year. It was a bet he won with some ease. He was well-connected, ambitious and creatively restless.

Woodley born, raised and schooled, with two guitar-playing elder brothers he opted to play the bass to avoid the comparisons and formed his first band, Warrior, whilst still at school, the highlight of their career being a "moving" performance from the back of a lorry as part of the 1974 Woodley Carnival.

The Voice, soon to be known as A Fast Crowd, with guitarist Steve Rolfe pictured on the right

A job at the following year's Festival allowed him to witness the set that stole the show from the crowd-swelling prog headliners that year, Yes. Dr Feelgood's stripped-down rhythm and blues won a legion of new fans that day and massively impressed the young Steve. Paving the way for the arrival of the Sex Pistols in a little over a year, here was an opportunity for him to forge a musical identity different from that of his Rolling Stones-loving brothers.

Like Trash, Steve spotted the advert looking for bands to audition for *Quadrophenia*, and with just a few tweaks in personnel Warrior became the suitably mod-sounding outfit, The Voice. He still has the rejection letter! No matter. Having seen a performance by punk minimalists Gang of Four at the University, a few more tweaks, a switch to playing guitar and The Voice became the more indie sounding A Fast Crowd. The band fitted well with Nick Duckett's Monday Club adventurers, eventually emerging as the A1 Vegetables, a fluid, flexible collective of souls, heavy on the percussion and electronics, the heartbeat of the band being provided by a primitive and often troublesome rhythm box removed from a Bontempi-style organ and referred to as Alice. At their first gig, a *Grinding Halt* benefit at the University, Alice flatly refused to cooperate. On her better days she underpinned the sound of heavy dub bass and unusual and unexpected guitar fills, keeping the beat steady under the layers of added percussion. Musicians appeared when they were available, but all were interchangeable, except Steve himself and his long-time musical and fanzine collaborator Greg Pope. Part of the notorious Pop Records Magnifico Mystery Tour, their finest hour arrived as support to The Thompson Twins, again at the University, which found both bands on stage performing a spectacular percussive work-out.

A spell with The Ballistics included a chance to play in the home of dub and reggae in the town, Central Club. Understandably nervous, this was like The Rolling Stones taking their English version of R'n'B back to its roots in Chicago. It went well, but for the fact that Steve, in his enthusiasm, jumped down from the stage to mingle with the admittedly sparse crowd and was unable to climb back up, humiliatingly having to unplug and walk around to the side.

Next up, he formed a duo with bassist Gary Jones from El Seven over a shared love of country music and 50s rock and roll. They called themselves Lost Weekend, Steve buying an old-school Hofner f-hole guitar and Gary a bright red double bass, setting out with the avowed intention of playing every pub in Reading. They may even have come close. A gig supporting Mic and Alison's Friction Groove at Harlesden's Mean Fiddler had them included on the list of the best bands to play the venue in 1986. This was some compliment and came about by including in their set a country weepie by George Jones, titled 'He Stopped Loving Her Today', which just happened to be venue owner Vince Power's favourite song! This, of course, was the same man who would later take control of the Reading Festival. Positive music press and prestigious support slots followed, but a less-than-successful flexi-disc release, financially speaking, saw the impetus of the duo peter out and, as ever, they moved on.

Steve had been a great fan of Gary's band El Seven, the core of which was Gary himself and fellow Merseysider John Townsend, both having moved down south in the mid-70s. Their potential was spotted by the mighty United Artists organisation, who signed

Gary Jones and Steve Rolfe of Lost Weekend, at Woodcray Studio

John Townsend recording with Movita in the same studio

them up and then promptly dropped them when a takeover by EMI prompted the inevitable clear-out. Picked up by Nick Duckett, the two singles his Pop Records label released feature strong melodies and driving bass lines, the keyboards of Jon Hoskins pulling their new wave/punky sound close to Elvis Costello's Attractions or their fellow Liverpudlians, The Yachts. One of the strongest contributions to the compilation *Beyond The River* is also theirs: 'Under Control'. Another talented outfit that the gods declined to favour, it had all looked so promising when they supported Ultravox at The Marquee and Siouxsie and The Banshees in a skinhead-blighted show in High Wycombe, but after the Pop Records Magnifico Tour they packed it in, Gary becoming half of Lost Weekend and John and, er Jon, forming the more synth-inclined Movita. Once again, they had some excellent tunes, one of the best of them, 'Love From Johnny', was released as a twelve inch single and is today highly collectable. It also has the distinction of being covered by Dave Berry on his *Hostage to The Beat* LP and for which John also contributed guitar.

Back on Merseyside, John's still performing and even includes some of the old El Seven stuff in his sets. About his time down South he says

"They were great times… but I don't miss it. That was then and this is now."

Also on the Criminal Damage compilation from 86 is a solo track by Gary Jones titled 'Walking to America' which compiler Chris Green described as a piece of "genius multi-tracked acapella." Lyrically it pines for a world far away from the bar of one of his favourite haunts, The Rose and Thistle, yearning for the land that gave birth to the music he loved. This was the sound of what might have been, perhaps, because he sadly died far too young a man back in 2007.

A lover of close harmonies, he'd also been much in demand as a bass player, joining Mike Cooper's 80s ensemble Continental Drift. Appearing at a jazz and blues festival in Paris alongside Chuck Berry, they were approached by the great man to be his backing band for the night, minus Mike Cooper.

The two components only met up an hour before the show, Steve Rolfe witnessing the union and thinking that the two elements fitted perfectly together. Gary clearly felt that Chuck's guitar was a little out of tune and approached the man who basically invented rock guitar and offered to lend him his tuner. As his jaw hit the floor, Chuck turned to the piano player Pat Thomas and said, "Did that boy just call me a n*****?"

Nobody, but nobody got to tell Mr Chuck Berry that his guitar might need a tune!

Always Mighty: The Ballistics

They were originally The Ballistics, then The Mighty Ballistics, then added the Hi-Power, and then reduced it to MB Hi-Power. However it was written, everybody knew who you were talking about. This crew were one of the most impressive and arguably one of the most important acts to come out of the Reading area during the 1980s.

Fuelled by a righteous anger directed squarely at the Tory government, it might be assumed that the band were not exactly a bundle of laughs, their publicity photos suggesting that they took themselves very seriously indeed. And why should they not? They felt they had something to contribute, expressed their forthright opinions in an original fashion and played music you could dance to. And unlike so many of their contemporaries, were refreshingly honest about their own backgrounds. This is Chris Maund quoted in the fanzine *Exposure*:

> "The majority of us in the band come from wealthy backgrounds. That doesn't matter. It's nothing to be ashamed of... you should never try and hide your past. Anyway, it always comes creeping back up on you in time."

Chris Green signed them up to his Criminal Damage label claiming that he'd never heard anything else like them. Visually, theirs was a classic British take on working class rockabilly style, pure Gene Vincent's Blue Caps. They then added some heavy, heavy dub bass, a chopping, echoed guitar and a Strummer-like sense of suppressed fury, the rolling r's and Doom Town vocal tones the icing on the top. Their mixed heritage gave them added relevance and better reflected the rising 80s face of a changing Britain that seemed to be so much under threat. Their music came with uncompromising lyrics with titles like, '4 Million On The Dole', 'Justice For The Poor', and

The Mighty Ballistics Hi-Power 12-inch mini LP from 1986 on Criminal Damage

the single, 'Springheel Jack', which deals with rape and the multitude of injustices suffered by women. Reviewing a gig at The Majestic in August 1986, Sounds had this to say:

> "it's only when you get really close to them that you feel the sincere power of their anger."

They were rightly impressed, but it didn't mean that their records were selling in any great quantity, despite the use of the logo from Roger Moore's TV series, The Saint. Perhaps they weren't prepared to make the compromises necessary to make hit records, because, believe me, all the ingredients were right there.

The Mad, The Moody and The Magnificent

...and not necessarily in that order. Diatribe were Spot The Dog's rhythm section, Jonathan and Tim Kirby, drums and bass respectively, a duo that pre-dated the White Stripes and Royal Blood by thirty years. Signed to Criminal Damage, the duo produced a stunning four-track EP that is relentless in its intensity, paranoid in vision and gothic in its execution. It is strong stuff, the final track's repeated climactical phrase, "Ha, fucking, ha!" has Tim hollering with an impossible-to-supress anger and despair that makes that master of confrontational intensity, Henry Rollins, sound about as intimidating as Nik Kershaw.

In performance they were almost frightening to behold, and seemingly conceived to implode, spectacularly. As a more than ill-judged attention-seeking publicity stunt, they burst into the offices of the *NME* and fired a couple of blank shots over the receptionist's head. Neither the police nor the editor of the paper were amused in the slightest, killing off any chance of promotion for the newly released record and sounding the death knell for the band, but, oh boy! They were an impressive outfit, and well ahead of their times.

Keyboard wizard Mark Hawkins spent a year gigging with The Complaints before deciding to team up with his brother once more and launch Jo Jo Namoza. Highly proficient musicians, they created frenetic, rhythm-driven, danceable worldbeat songs coupled with politically savvy lyrics. What Mark had brought back with him was a realisation that a strong, visual presence was essential to getting an act noticed. To this end, they recruited Dublin-born Francis Magee, who quickly proved to be an inspired choice.

Magee exuded charisma, mixing mime with some extraordinary monologues between numbers. His was a mesmerising, winning presence that set the band apart, making them a powerhouse of a live band and a very hard act to follow, as I can tell you from experience.

They released one excellent single towards the end of the 80s, 'Kissing The Babies', which helped to get the band noticed across the South East. And they made three trips to Norway, for the first of which the band were met at the airport by a stretch limo!

Unfortunately, Magee departed to become a very successful film and television actor, appearing for two years in *EastEnders*, innumerable other roles that included *Game of Thrones*, and film

Diatribe's Ha, Fucking Ha!

credits for *Layer Cake*, *The Dig* and a dozen others. Good for him, but a shame for the band, because they really were very good indeed.

The Gathering came out of Henley during the mid-80s and worked harder than almost anyone else on the circuit for their success. Veering towards the gothic, the tracks they contributed to two local compilation LPs are among the best on offer there, the song, 'Splash', a heartbreaker of a number, is so good they re-recorded it for their eponymous album, released in 1986. With its arresting cover art, the record deserves to be as collectable as it has become. As is the 12-inch single, 'Rant', a fast goth meets punk piece of action released on their own Final Records. Do yourself a favour and dig out what they left behind. Their material has certainly travelled. I picked up a copy of their LP in a shop in Utah!

10. Pick up the Pieces

We Came, We Saw, and We Had A Good Time

With the notable exceptions of the University, Bulmershe College and the Tech, music venues opened and closed across the town with bewildering rapidity and there were few constants throughout the period. The closing of the Top Rank in early 1983 and its conversion to bingo robbed the town of a comfortable, decent-sized performance space that had accommodated the aspirations of a wide range of promoters over the years, and from the late 70s had seemingly hosted everybody from Joy Division to Gladys Knight and the Pips. The Hexagon opened for business at the tail-end of 1977 and Tim Hulse, the venue's first General Manager, certainly set the bar high for those that followed, the first few years featuring a stellar lineup of talent that ranged across all genres whilst also managing to squeeze in local band showcases and Saturday lunchtime performances for the area's rising stars. And standards remained high for the rest of the 80s, 1987's eclectic offerings, for instance, included Motörhead, Misty in Roots, The Communards, Ben E King and Billy Joe Spears.

A postcard view of the Hexagon from the IDR, 1980

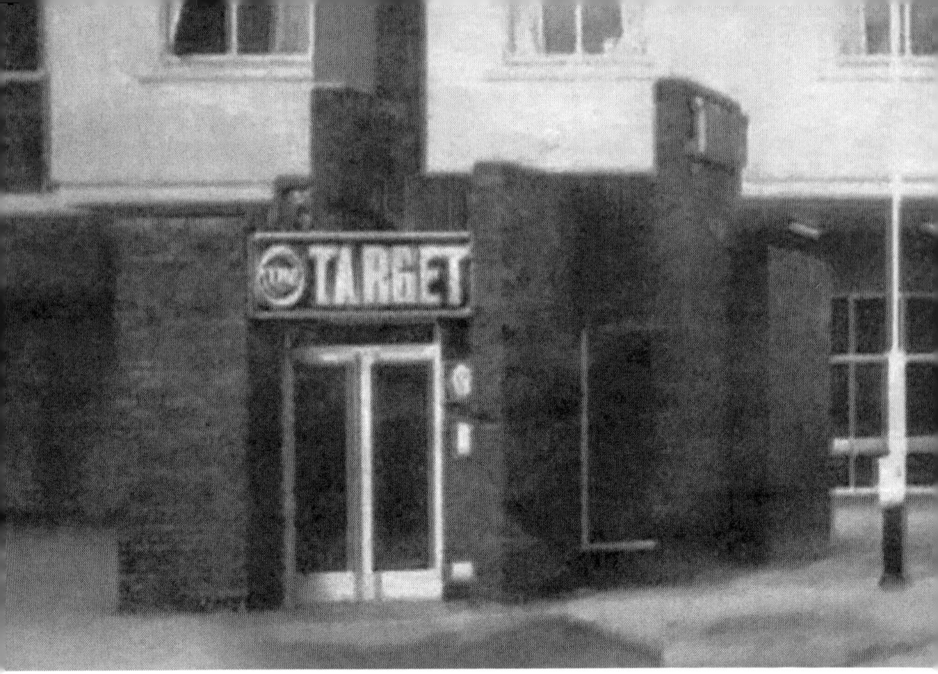
TARGET

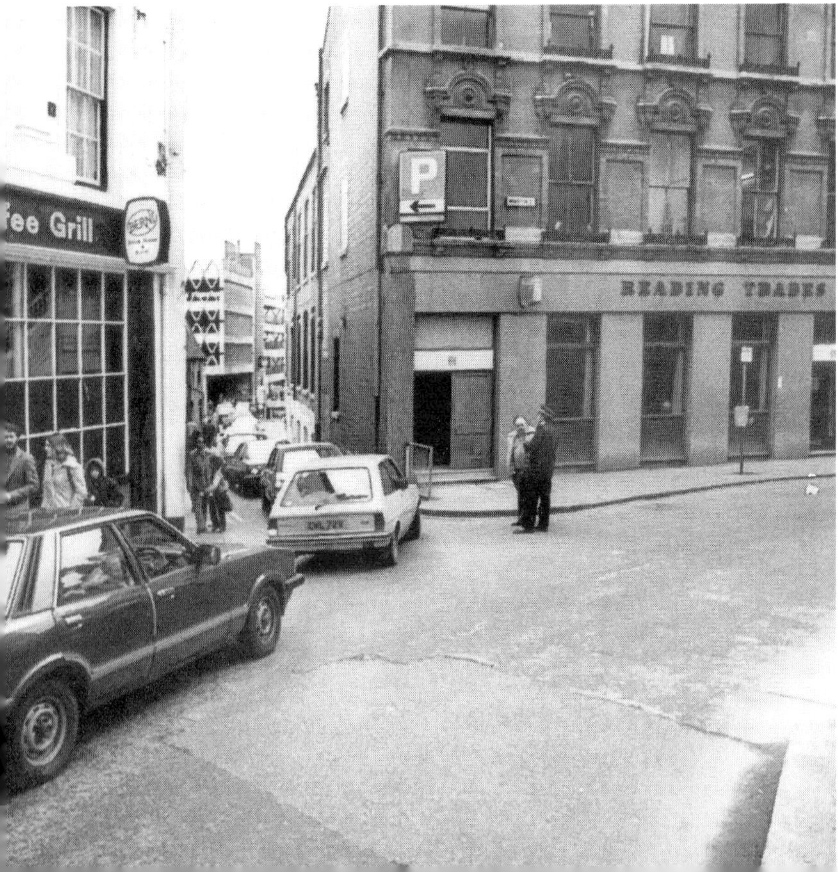
fee Grill
P
READING TRADES

Some of the venues around Reading that hosted live music:
The Target, in the Butts Shopping Centre; the Reading Trades Union Club, Minster Street; The Crown, Caversham

Undoubtedly the loss of The Target was a blow in the mid-80s. Armed with the knowledge that there was live music on six nights a week people like Mick Brock would often just turn up to see what was happening. Cherry's Wine Bar, situated in a concrete terrace of shops and restaurants opposite the station and long-since demolished, fulfilled a similar role, although, as Mick found, its clientele of squaddies, punks and skins on busy nights often proved to be a volatile mixture. Nervous as to how we would go down with this audience when The Complaints played there in 1981, I was rather relieved when we finished the first number to a complete and rather eerie silence save for the sound of pool balls being potted way back in the shadows.

Fives Bar was in the Butts Centre, opposite The Hexagon. Smarter than Cherry's (where wasn't?), it hosted the area's finest for a couple of years before morphing into The New Yorker and choosing to live a quieter life. High Wycombe-educated Howard Jones played Fives in 1982 in front of an audience of very modest proportions. Three years later he was playing Wembley, Live Aid and the world.

The Three Tuns, The Merry Maidens, The Britannia Tap, and every pub, Union or Church Hall from Emmer Green to Whitley Street hosted noisy, live music, often after being persuaded to do so by the likes of Nick Duckett. There was so much variety on offer, and so much interest in it that a good crowd was almost guaranteed.

The Cap and Gown opposite the Tech College hosted the John Barleycorn Folk Club for a while, presenting acts as prestigious as Martin Carthy and Michael Chapman in the early 80s, and a lot more besides, as it became a place that made you feel that all had not been lost with the closing of The Target. Here, though, there was even more variety. The Pandemonium Club, for example, arrived from the back room of The Crown and was dedicated to improvised and experimental music. Reading legend Mike Cooper was a regular contributor, as was saxophonist Tim Hill. Not everybody's cup of tea, but then neither is punk or metal.

It was also the home of Damian Clarke's Pressgang Club, determined to bring folk music kicking and screaming into a post-punk world. The club was either an abomination or a breath of fresh air, depending on how you liked your folk music served up, I guess. By

The George Hotel, King Street

the late 80s The George Hotel and The Caversham Bridge Hotel were hosting the likes of June Tabor and John Renbourn in what were probably regarded as more traditional surroundings.

Central Club was forced out of its original home in Chain Street provoking protracted protests, but it eventually found a new home in the ex-police garage at the bottom of London Street and continued to promote the best reggae music to be heard west of London. Aswad, Prince Far I, Freddie McGregor and a host of other stars featured regularly, as did local heroes Urban Warrior and The Duncans.

Paradise Club promoter Tony Long remembers going out as a teenager in Reading and feeling distinctly unwelcome when catching a performance by reggae duo Clint Eastwood and General Saint at Central in the early 80s. He likened walking past the club in Chain Street to walking past a crowd of skinheads; there seemed to be this sense that at any moment he was going to get clobbered. Of course, both groups of youths had found powerful cultural identity through music and jealously guarded what they deemed to be their turf against outsiders. Even working as sound engineers at reggae gigs or skinhead punk shows could be a stressful business.

For the skinheads there was the sense that white, working-class culture and the jobs associated with it were under attack and disappearing fast. I'm sure I don't need to go through all the reasons why reggae music had become such a powerful symbol of cultural expression for black youth in the late 70s and 80s. This is ours, white boy, they seemed to be saying. Respect that and keep out.

I wish that it hadn't been like that, but it was. The story of Central Club and the incredible list of reggae and dub stars who performed there is waiting to be written by somebody who was involved. I wouldn't suggest that we are living in a perfect world today, but we're moving in the right direction, surely?

From the middle of the decade The Granby in Cemetery Junction opened as a live music venue and often featured acts in the very early stages of their existence. With live music featured most nights of the week it became the first stopping place on a Friday or Saturday night musical tour of the town. If she wasn't gigging herself, Jo Morris, Great Mistakes bass player, was out supporting friends and sizing up the opposition:

"It was a great live music scene. It wasn't just about lending support; we just loved to see our contemporaries and knew we'd bump into loads of friends."

The bands came on early at The Granby. You could catch most of a set before charging up the road for a quick pint in The Turks Head or catch somebody's acoustic set next door in The Boozy Blues Bar. Closing time and it was down to The Majestic or across the road to The Paradise Club for the main event of the evening. And throughout all this time that place was the one constant, 112 London Street, the former dance studio hidden behind an unprepossessing door down a short, poorly lit alley. It had gone under half a dozen different names during the 60s and 70s but by the end of the decade had settled on being The Caribbean Club, a musical and cultural haven for the Windrush generation where the beer was cheap and dominoes had almost developed into a contact sport. It changed into The Paradise Club in the early 80s with a host of people promoting there, including the legendary Pogle, and then The After Dark in the late 80s, finally closing its doors only a couple of years back. The black painted walls would be dripping with condensation, the air thick with smoke, the temperature oppressive, the sound levels debilitating and the crush at the bar five deep. On a good night there was nowhere like it to listen and dance to live music. Angie's, a converted barn at the Cantley House Hotel in Wokingham, gave it a run for its money, as did Bracknell's Cellar Bar, but were both much smaller and lacked The Paradise Club's late-night frisson.

Here Comes Johnny Reggae

In punk's younger days it was not unusual to find punk and reggae acts playing alongside one another, Johnny Rotten famously helping to cement the bond by wearing a badge celebrating those Birmingham-raised reggae warriors Steel Pulse, this sense of solidarity born in troubled times even inspiring Bob Marley to write his song 'Punky Reggae Party'.

By the 80s tribalism in music had become more pronounced, the separation between musical styles reflected in the town's pubs and clubs, but perhaps most obviously at the Festival, where reggae bands in particular could expect a tough time. No wonder Central

Club could appear unwelcoming to outsiders. There were those that refused to accept this move towards musical separatism, The Mighty Ballistics being one such. But there were others.

Reading reggae stars Urban Warrior saw it as their mission to try and bridge the gap between cultures. When interviewed by *Red Rag* back in 82 they were a nine-piece outfit, star man Aqua Livi being a member for a time. He, of course, went on to have an illustrious career as a solo artist and band leader well into the new century.

Regularly appearing at Central Club, The Paradise, The Hexagon and the University, they also gigged much further afield, taking in the Notting Hill Carnival and even travelling to Africa and the Sudan, where they were one of the first foreign bands to play in the country. Putting their principles into action, they headlined an evening of otherwise post-punk fare at the West End Centre in Aldershot with which I was involved and the only time I got to share a stage with them. Frankly, they wiped the floor with us all musically, but the band members continued to greet me as a long-lost friend on the streets of Reading for years after.

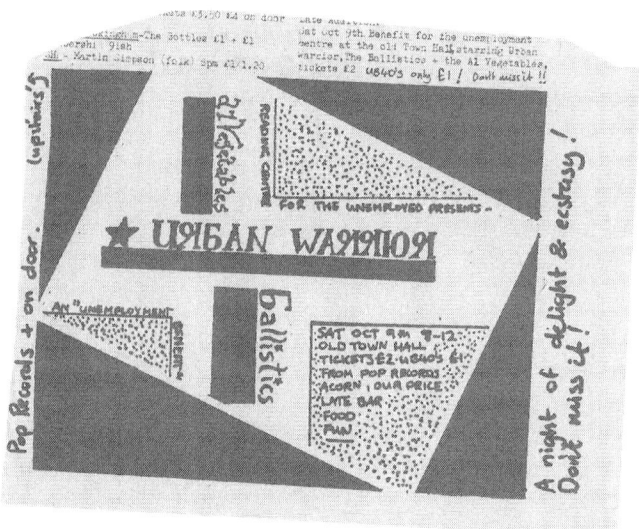

Urban Warrior starred at a Benefit for the Unemployed Centre at the Town Hall on 9 October 1982

They played their own material, the lyrics often reflecting the plight of black people in the UK. They had this to say to *Red Rag*'s interviewer:

> "Reading has the same problems as any other place, it's just that it's one of the more affluent areas… With the education system, housing etc we think black people suffer the brunt of these things. Working class whites have the same problems but we think that being black adds to those problems."

And just why was Central Club so jealously guarded?

> "It is important that blacks have their own place to express what they feel, hence the importance of these places."

Sadly, nothing was ever released by the band. They stuck to their principles, but it seems an unfortunate decision to have made:

> "As far as the majors go, a lot of fun would be taken away from making our music because of compromise. We play a certain style, but the record company's view is, right, we need to change this, and the result is someone else's work."

You can't get more hard-core punk in attitude than that.

Also refusing to be pigeon-holed, reggae stars Misty in Roots played Bones in June 1978. In support were El Seven and a group calling themselves The Duncans. Five members of the same family of second-generation Caribbean immigrants living in Reading, four brothers and sister Gracie, an Alfred Sutton student. Having recorded a couple of tracks at Audiogenic they had been spotted by the owners of a Wokingham jazz record business, Ian Gilkes and Peter Woollet, who took the tracks to the London-based Sound News Studios, a company that specialised in turning out private pressings.

The resulting single, 'Blackbird (part 1)', is a fine piece of late 70s melodic reggae in the style of artists like The Mighty Diamonds. The reverse side, a dub version of the same number, is even better, the frantic, echoed percussion and solo guitar swooping in and out of the busy mix and driven on by the relentless bass. Sadly, this excellent piece of work didn't manage to prolong their career and they disappear from the gig lists soon afterwards. The tracks are, of course, available online, and are an absolute treat, but you'll have to pay a small fortune for an original copy.

11. Never Trust the Weather

Am-Aid

Concerts come no bigger nor more famous than the one that took place at the old Wembley Stadium on 13 July 1985, Live Aid. At the mid-point of a decade now chiefly remembered for almost succeeding in turning greed into a virtue, the nation's conscience had been pricked by a famine in East Africa that was daily turning from being a catastrophe into the actual Apocalypse before our eyes. The concert's unprecedented success as a fundraising event, propelled by Bob Geldof's hectoring intensity, made us all want to do our bit and organising local concerts was as good a way as any to raise money for the cause.

Two fundraisers for Live Aid were organised in the town, the first, at The Paradise Club, was put together by Mic Dover and Alison Rolls of Friction Groove, Steve Rolfe of Lost Weekend and his bandmate Gary's partner, Katie, and took place about two weeks after the Wembley and Philadelphia extravaganzas. The line-up consisted of Friction Groove and Lost Weekend, of course, the fabulous Mighty Ballistics Hi-Power, The Scanners and, because they needed a band to pull in those punters when the pubs had shut, The Complaints. Scan PA Hire agreed to do the gig for free, and the only person who had to be paid that night was the Paradise Club cleaner, the manager saying that he just couldn't ask the old chap to do it for nothing! A raffle was organised, the place was rammed, and a fun-packed evening raised around eleven hundred quid for the cause. Full marks to the organisers. That's the way to do it.

The second concert, a far more ambitious affair, was scheduled for mid-September, a full two months after the big one, and, like Geldof and Midge Ure's extravaganza, had big ambitions. In prospect were a single, a video and an all-day outdoor musical event featuring mostly local talent and staged at Reading's Smallmead Stadium, with the promise of a lot of big star involvement along the way.

The idea for the fundraising single, 'Wake Up World', seems to have originated with Wayne Hunt, who took the idea to Danny Fraifeld of The Geisha Girls, who then roped in Clive Hacker and Jo Morris of The Great Mistakes. The resulting song had potential, said all the right things and was very catchy.

Reading Am-Aid poster, 1985

It was left to Wayne to sort out the concert, Clive to organise the recording of the single and the video, and Danny and Sprog to act as scroungers for the entire enterprise. Right from the start they persuaded BT to give them £600 worth of phone use and a state-of-the-art DEC computer, although nobody had any idea what to do with this. Martin Rushent's studio in Goring proved a useful place to get hold of phone numbers for the stars, the duo returning home to find that a housemate had already taken down a message from some chap offering his services called David Gilmour.

Gerry Anderson of Thunderbirds fame generously gave time in his Bray studios to record the single, and a sound stage to shoot the video. The finished recording featured a host of local talent backing the Pink Floyd legend, plus Ray Dorset of Mungo Jerry, and Page

Three pin-ups (this is the 8os, remember!) Linda Lusardi, Sam Fox and Angie Lane on backing vocals. Part of the accompanying video was shot in the Forbury Gardens where, according to the official Am-Aid press release:

> "Old ladies can be seen singing alongside punks. Babies, tramps and dogs are all featured."

As were the Mayor of Reading Mr Brian Fowles, Gilmour, Dorset, the aforementioned glamour girls (still in the 8os!), Reading F.C. players and a multitude of local musicians and singers.

A lot of people had put a huge amount of work into the project and the single and video were all set for release into an expectant world. Pink Floyd had even lent their back-line stage amplification for the live jamboree.

Unfortunately, the weather on the day of the concert was utterly appalling: driving rain and strong winds of the type that got D-Day postponed for twenty-four hours. Nobody was going to stand about and listen to music in those conditions, and consequently very few did. Determined Page Three Girls were photographed dutifully wearing their 'Wake Up World' t-shirts and the bands all played on into the teeth of the storm. It brightened up a little towards the end, the crowd having swollen to a few hundred brave, shivering souls, and closing act Mungo Jerry's up-beat happy vibes at least sent them home a little happier.

The single was never released, but the video was distributed to around eight hundred video jukeboxes across the country, a pub fad that barely outlasted the decade. There was also some unpleasantness around who had actually agreed to offer their services for free and who had not. Cooperation was replaced by incrimination and a desire of some to distance themselves quickly from the whole soggy enterprise. Says Sprog today:

> "There was an awful lot of strange ego stuff going on when some people worked out that they might be on the news the next day."

Did the whole business make any money for Geldof's cause? Does anybody know?

With a bit more luck it could have been a spectacular success. The fact that it was a complete disaster shouldn't detract from the fact that a lot of people put an immense amount of hard work into the project, and their intentions were honourable. For the most part. Sprog tells the story of visiting Dave Gilmour at his palatial residence and found the ace guitarist to be most accommodating, although Sprog did have to work hard to suppress his inner K9:

> "We went to this manor house and had a cup of tea. I went for a piss and down by the toilet were all these gold discs. One flick to the left and I could have pissed all over Pink Floyd! I didn't though coz he'd just made us cheese and tomato sandwiches!"

Clive Hacker has kept a book of press cuttings from the time. There's a Reading Am-Aid official sticker on the front which has been altered to read, The Reading Am-Aid Nightmare, and which probably sums it all up pretty well. That said, he did get to play guitar alongside one of his heroes!

Not The Reading Festival

The NJF/Marquee Organisation's annual bash was not the only large-scale musical event taking place in the town through the 70s and 80s, although, of course, it was far and away the biggest. That man Nick Duckett had organised outdoor events at Brock Barracks in the summers of 1980 and 1981 under his Monday Club banner, the first organised with the West Reading Community Association and billed as The Alternative Reading Festival. The Chief Constable even turned up for the first one and was, according to Nick, surprisingly affable, bearing in mind that there were people lounging all over the grass soaking up the good vibes and smoking, er, grass.

Anarchist groups were very active across the Borough during this time and generally in a positive, creative way, with the Acorn Bookshop, an establishment sympathetic to political alternatives, its intellectual epicentre underneath the Chatham Street multi-storey. Occupying abandoned factories and cinemas they enabled musical events to happen, often over prolonged time periods. With bursts of feverish activity, stages would be erected, equipment borrowed, and the word put out on the street. Our friend Nick Duckett was heavily involved in one such project, the "occupation" of the abandoned Granby cinema in Cemetery Junction in 1981 which held out against the forces of the law for two weeks. But probably the biggest of these took place in the redundant Earley Power Station in September 1985

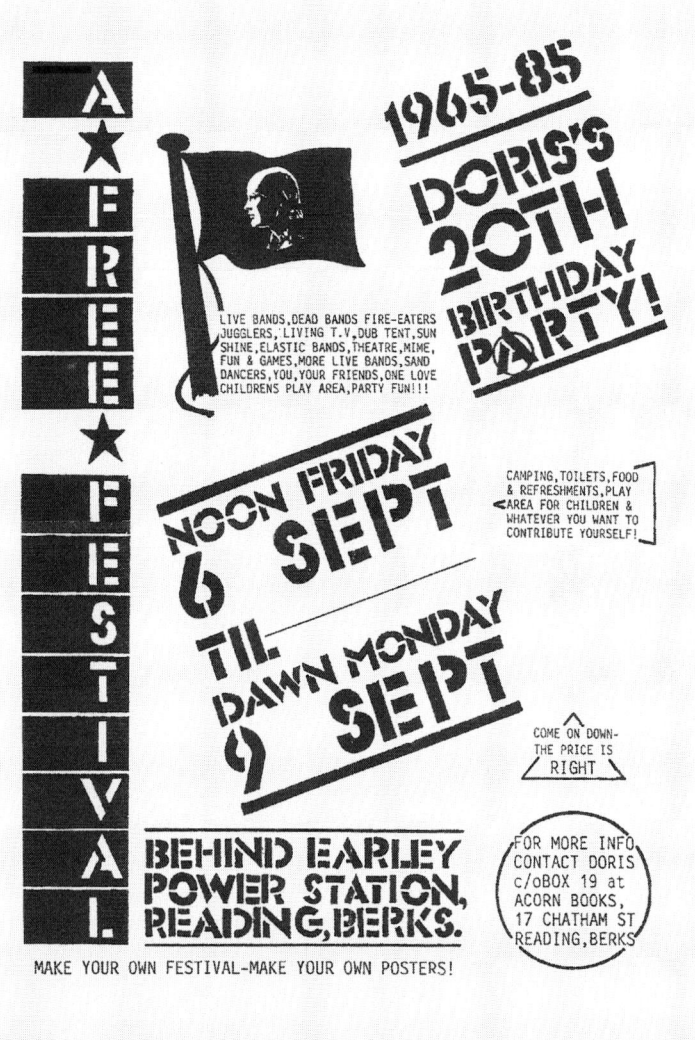

Doris's 20th Birthday Party

and was billed as Doris's 20th Birthday Party, a name thought less likely to promote controversy than The Anarchists' Free Festival, the saga of the Peace Convoy and the notorious Battle of the Beanfield with its reports of the heavy-handed actions of the police still fresh in people's minds. The Birthday Party advertised a camp site, food stalls, bars, children's play areas and even a first-aid post.

And all went well. A host of bands offered their services, among them those extollers of hippie virtues Here And Now, Ozric Tentacles, local heroes The Gathering and many, many more. *Red Rag*'s review referred to the fabulous weather, the great music and the abundance of friendly people, and had this to say, as Beat and the Devil brought Sunday night to an unforgettable climax:

> "a few young men were demonically but methodically smashing up piles of old televisions and dragging their entrails onto a large bonfire nearby. It was a very special weekend."

Hmm. James Carter, of Soft Dogs fame recalled that most people were so stoned that the whole thing seemed to be like some massive drugs party. Maybe. I was asked if I could loan the organisers some sound equipment, which I did with a rather heavy heart, only half expecting to see it again. But returned it was, in perfect order, and with a quarter ounce of Morocco's finest taped to the top in payment! Fair play to the anarchists, and happy birthday Doris!

Mud, Blood, and Chaos: Reading Festival 1977–79

The bulbs, biscuits and brewing industries of Reading have been gone for forty years now and the football club is back languishing in the third tier of English football, but the annual music festival goes from strength to strength, these days attracting over a hundred thousand paying guests to its riverside location. It's changed, of course. The peaceful scenes of the early 70s, the audience sprawled across the arena wreathed in cannabis smoke and dodging coppers gave way to the aggression of the late 70s and the beer-fuelled intolerance of the 80s. It still has its issues, of course, and these are gleefully dissected by both the local and national media.

I attended the Festival from the time of its arrival in the town in 1971 right up to the mid-90s, first as a punter, then from the mid-70s onwards as a front-stage security guard. There was no training given, the only stipulation being that we must not turn up drunk. Or stoned.

The early years were easy. Everybody sat about in friendship groups, standing only when darkness engulfed the arena, and the headliners took to the stage. We chatted to punters, swapped ciggies and cans of beer and hauled out the occasional tearful fan when the crush against the barriers became too much for them.

Mud at Reading Festival 1977

In 1977, the combination of some appallingly wet weather and the unleashing of punk into the UK's musical smorgasbord meant that the atmosphere was radically changed. The arena had been turned into marshland before the punters arrived, a shallow lake stretching out in all directions just waiting for those thousands of feet to turn it into a morass. It didn't take long. Mixed with vast quantities of beer, chips, pizza, vomit and urine, by Saturday the stench was unbearable. It was impossible to sit down and the audience's only salvation seemed to lie with the consumption of vast quantities of alcohol, and with such huge stores of ammunition to hand, the can fights were both spectacular and bloody. Plastered from head to toe in the toxic goo, more and more punters begged us to lift them over the barriers to escape before either hypothermia or a fractured cranium required hospitalisation.

In the year of punk there was precious little of it on the bill, only the spectacular failure of Wayne County to establish a rapport with the audience, but then, squeezed in between the Bob Calvert-era Hawkwind and the desperately needed Californian sunshine provided by The Doobie Brothers he/she never stood a chance. County was the embodiment of pure punk sleaze, like Lily Savage on crack, assertive and confrontational. Singer and band were pelted with anything the crowd could lay its hands on from the moment they took to the stage, amazingly braving the storm for a few numbers before accepting that it wasn't a fair contest and bolting for cover. County, defiant to the last, called us all a bunch of limey cocksuckers before departing to the loudest cheer of the afternoon. The 1977 Reading Festival was a tough place to be a punk.

It was a festival to be endured, and there were casualties. One poor chap clung to the barriers caked with mud, soaked to the skin and very much the worse for wear. We inquired after his welfare several times and his thumbs-up indicated that he was ok. There were thousands out there just like him, to be fair. As the crowd dispersed at the end of the day, he didn't. Medics were called but it was too late to save him. A tragic end to a miserable weekend.

Rather like the town itself, it took until the following year for the Festival to acknowledge the arrival of punk and the new wave, and the Friday night was given over to it. The Jam topped the bill that night, with support from those superior pub rock veterans The Pirates, the wonderful Pauline Murray-fronted Penetration and Sham 69, whose singer Jimmy Pursey was at this time the go-to guy for seemingly endless quotes about the state of the nation's youth. Oh, and they had by this time attracted a hardcore right-wing skinhead following.

Half an hour before the band were due on stage a large knot of these guys had muscled their way through the crowd and up to the front. My security team melted away, and as the band took to the stage two hundred skins vaulted over the barrier, dispensed with the meagre security that remained and clambered onto the stage where they joined with their heroes, and the band's slightly surprising guest guitarist, Steve Hillage. Frankly, little damage had been done, but the era of the old hippie days of security by consent had been well and truly buried.

Patti Smith closed the weekend on the Sunday as the crowds drifted away. An inspired choice, she was arty without being aloof,

Punk and new wave arrive at the Festival, 1978

punky without being nihilistic and the embodiment of the inclusive spirit of the new age, the Festival was thus neatly dovetailed by contrasting takes on the New Music. A cartoon band really, Sham garnered their substantial support from the overwhelmingly male, conservative element within the white working class. Patti Smith, of course, swung with the left and appealed to both students and their teachers with her more cerebral approach. No "we're going down the pub" type lyrics for this gal, but punk was always about both these approaches.

Spooked by the ease with which the barricades were breached in 1978 but unwilling to ditch the softly-softly approach to security altogether, Festival organisers took two courses of action for the following year, 1979: they ditched the idea of turning over an entire day's programming to the new wave, scattering the few they'd booked among the mainstream rock acts across the entire weekend. They

Molly Hatchet on stage at the Festival in 1979. Fine Southern rockers; hairy to the point of parody

also hired a specialist back-up security team should they be required. Lovely guys, those Belgian muscle men. They kept a low profile, but when summoned quickly extinguished all signs of aggression simply by being huge.

As for the music, The Cure provided welcome relief from some pretty stodgy performances on the Friday, and everybody got to see why The Police were becoming enormous very quickly. Molly Hatchet seemed ludicrously hairy for the times and local boys (Camberley, local-ish) The Members, thwarted with some panache concerted efforts by the crowd to use them as target practice:

"Get with the fucking times, will you? It's 1979!"

retorted singer Nicky Tesco. And as the only real punk band on an otherwise conservative rock bill, staying the course and finishing their set was quite the achievement.

Good Evening Reading! The Festival from 1980

After the troubles of 1978 and some sporadic fighting between metal and new wave fans in 1979, the 1980 festival opted for a booking policy that was heavy metal almost all the way, some of it old-school like Gillan, Gary Moore and Whitesnake, but a lot of it NWBHM, with Def Leppard and Iron Maiden poised to break big. Most of the others were stalwarts of the Marquee Club in the process, as they say in rock circles, of paying their dues. Only true believers could tell them apart. On they would bounce, all leopard skin and spandex, blow-dried and bouffant. Good Evening Reading! It was barely one o' clock in the afternoon.

Each band's acolytes would be gathered in a knot up front, an easy feat to achieve in the early afternoon, but much, much harder as the day wore on and crowd density increased in anticipation of the evening's headliners. Early performers played to a fraction of the numbers expected later and the arena would be a relatively

Whitesnake playing Reading Festival in 1980

Against The Grain opened the Festival in 1982

comfortable place to be. With the sun shining and a supply of beers to hand, movement out to the toilets was still possible, and with your flag flying high your mates would have no difficulty finding you later.

The pattern was set for the rest of the 80s. The organisers figured that metal was a safe bet and would pull in the fans, the NWBHM was flying high and metal in all its glorious forms was taking over the world. Further down the bill there might be some semblance of variety, although presenting a reggae band, in this case Steel Pulse in 1983, met with the same rabid reaction from the crowd as when it was first attempted back in 1976.

Still, at least some of those local acts who'd dutifully worked their way round the circuit were finally given the break they'd always dreamt about, and a chance to be able to say to their grandkids, "I played the Reading Festival".

Against The Grain, whose regular appearances at Cherry's and The Target invariably packed the places solid, got their chance to open

Twelfth Night during their second Reading Festival performance in 1983

the Festival in 1982, and, of course, Dog'ouse, and The Larry Miller Band in 1986. Twelfth Night appeared early doors on the Sunday of 1981, and again in 1983 when they were the second band to play on the Sunday, the crowd larger and a little more settled. And they earned themselves an encore!

There was a break for a couple of years, the Tory-controlled council surprisingly blocking this money-spinning enterprise for so many of the town's businesses, but it returned in 1986. In the interim, the NJF/Marquee organisation had sought to keep things ticking over by moving the whole shebang to Ilford, headlining with Jethro Tull on Saturday night. Twelfth Night would have appeared that day around five thirty, fourth on the bill, and when the arena would have been heaving with humanity. The event, of course, was never staged. It just might have been the show that propelled the band into the premier league, who knows?

Reading Festival: a money-spinner for many Reading businesses – not least of all The Moderation on Caversham Road

After I stopped working at the Festival in the mid-90s I continued to turn up as a punter every year until around 2010, when, looking about me shortly after arriving on site I realised that I was by far the oldest person amongst this sea of teenagers and felt rather awkward. It was time to call it a day. In 2012, my stepdaughter Mia, aged thirteen, was desperate to see Florence and The Machine and booked day tickets with a group of schoolfriends. Driving down the Caversham Road that day past the thousands of fans arriving on site took me right back to my first Reading in 1971, and that feeling of camaraderie brought about by a shared love for the event and the music. I sensed that same feeling in the excited chatter of my youthful passengers as we passed The Moderation and turned the corner into Richfield Avenue.

12. And Here Come the 90s

We started this story with a young Paul McColm returning from Australia to a UK musical landscape that had been transformed by punk and having been raised in a musical household where it was not unusual to find people like Georgie Fame kipping on the family sofa, to say he was eager to get involved with the new scene is an understatement. He placed an advertisement in Pop Records and became the drummer for The Great Mistakes. It was that simple. And there was this whole generation of young people across the UK who did something similar. Locally, this eventually developed into what Phil Broadhurst was confident enough to refer to in his fanzine *Utterance* as The Thamesbeat Phenomenon.

Mic Dover's taste of the big time with Friction Groove never for him eclipsed those "hot, steamy nights" rocking in Cherry's Wine Bar. Tellingly, his favourite Friction Groove gig was the humble Live Aid fundraiser at The Paradise Club. And two-time Reading Festival prog maestros Twelfth Night just loved playing Wokingham's Angie's Club, its tiny, narrow and intimate confines literally packed to the rafters.

But everything moves on. Venues close, the music changes, and a new generation seizes the reins of creativity. By 1987 the first Acid House raves were being reported in the press and ecstasy was becoming the drug of choice for those who wanted to dance till dawn, causing fits of anxiety and blanket condemnation in the press. Stock Aitken Waterman-penned material began to dominate the charts alongside Madonna and Michael Jackson, who continued their reign as the planet's biggest stars. Metal came back to earth with the unstoppable rise of Guns n' Roses, and just waiting to take over the world were Public Enemy and NWA, giving a voice to black disaffection that resonated around the globe and helped to propel hip hop into the most popular, effective and lucrative mode of musical expression on the planet.

There were two or three bands at the decade's end who should have been huge, if there ever was such a thing as musical justice, which of course there isn't. Home and Abroad's singer Darrell Mitchell had been blessed with a fine, deeply mellow voice and an ability to construct tunes with wickedly barbed hooks, ably assisted in their realisation by band-mates Barry Light on drums and Ian

Norrington on bass, who sadly died in an accident at the end of the 90s. Country boys from out Wallingford way, they rehearsed in the same hut as the Blewbury Brass Band, and cut their teeth playing numberless community centres, youth clubs and Masonic halls, all out in the sticks.

Yet another group who recorded with Martin Nichols, they featured almost weekly on Radio 210's *Off The Wall*, Barry the Fence being such a big fan that he eventually agreed to be their manager, coining the phrase the Tonka Toys of Pop to describe them. I think he meant they were compact and powerful! Berkshire's John Peel, as Darrell refers to him, also negotiated for them to be the first band signed to the then fledgling Spanish label Elefant Records.

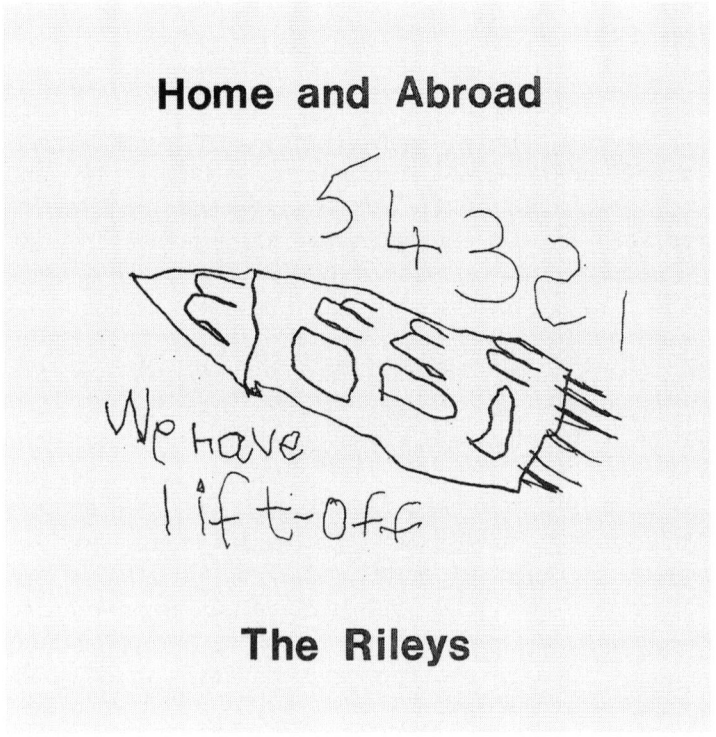

A flexi-disc release shared between The Rileys and Home and Abroad, with a track each

They released three singles, the marvellous 'Alison' in 1989, 'Smokey Town' in 1991 and 'Kennedy' in 1993, along with a cassette album and a shared flexi with The Rileys that featured their showstopper 'Big Red Bus'. All are very collectable today. Footage of the band performing live from The After Dark in 1991 reveals a cohesive musical unit that is indeed compact and powerful rockin' out to a crowd that's packed in and jumpin'!

The Rileys were from Woodley, as were Feverfew, the two bands swapping members with each other from time to time. Indie in their approach, both featured an arresting mix of male and female vocals and performed material tinged with a sweet, affecting innocence. Both bands released a series of singles from the end of the decade, their shared EP, *Happiness*, further cementing their bond. The Rileys had earlier teamed up for a flexi with Home and Abroad taking a track apiece and packaged within a very sweet cover depicting The Riley's guitarist as a lad. Let that boy boogie woogie!

And then it all began to happen at once, or so it seemed. International Resque, soon to be shortened to Resque, were among the first out of the blocks, packing out The Majestic in their early days with ex-Complaints drummer Alan Burgess behind the kit, who no doubt was feeling his age! They offered a sort of post-punk cabaret, according to The Evening Post's reviewer at the time, with plentiful distractions in the form of outrageous outfits and synchronised gymnastics. A joyous riot, in fact, full of 60s-influenced drive and humour, they released a couple of singles and the LP, *Life's A Bonus* to a grateful and rapidly expanding fan base gathered through constant hard work gigging across the nation. Sadly, the glorious future that seemed assured was only ever partly realised, leaving an awful lot of people wanting more but having to be content with the memories.

The Colour Mary likewise. A "noisy guitar band from Reading" is how they somewhat disingenuously describe themselves on their Facebook page, because they were so much more. Recording supremo Martin Nichols might have relocated to Weston-super-Mare but his reputation ensured that his former clients were happy to make the trip, The Colour Mary among them, recording most of the material on their EP releases with him. In 1990 Radio 1 aired a live performance from The Marquee Club and which is now available on various digital music platforms. Why weren't they huge?

The Colour Mary

The Heart Throbs, however, were. Formed in 1986 by two Reading students, the outfit expanded to a four-piece and included sisters Rose Carlotti and Rachel DeFreitas, whose brother Pete banged the drums for Echo & The Bunnymen. With regular appearances at The Caribbean and The Majestic, Chris Green included them on Criminal Damage's final release, a compilation, remarking later:

"How ironic that the last group on the last track of our last release would go on to be one of the most successful."

They were, but sadly not on his label. The track, 'Toy', was their first single, the sisters alternating vocals over a simple, driving, two-chord construction that allows the voices to carry the tune. The lyrics are smart too: girl looks for love, finds it, boy cheats, girl is disillusioned and gets hopping mad. And I mean, really, really angry. The mildly pornographic sleeve was unsettling rather than sexy, the message seeming to be, don't fuck with us, ok? Ok! They recorded three sensational albums before disbanding, carrying their punk legacy and their pride in their female sexual assertiveness out of the Valley and into the world.

Slowdive – one of the most successful bands to come out of Reading

The best band to come out of Reading?

For that accolade, however, there was now developing some serious competition. It is only a slight exaggeration to suggest that Chapterhouse and Slowdive invented a new rock genre, the shoegaze scene. Of course there were others, but both were immensely successful, Chapterhouse's 1991 album, Whirlpool, and Slowdive's Souvlaki from 1993 being seen as highlights of the genre, the latter as one of the strongest releases by a UK band in the 90s. Once again, Martin Nichols' involvement in their development should be noted, but the full story of their rise to becoming internationally recognised musical brand leaders will have to wait for volume three!

It had been thirteen years since The Sex Pistols and, unwittingly, Bill Grundy, unleashed a musical rebellion across the nation and fanned the flames of creative discontent in the suburbs of Whitley and Calcot. And then finally, right at the end of the decade, the breakout from the Valley so long expected finally happened. Big time.

Stand Up and Be Counted: Reading Bands 1977–1987

This list of performers has been compiled from information published in the national music press, local newspapers, gig guides, flyers, diaries and an ageing memory.

There are bound to be mistakes and omissions, for which I am very sorry, and some of these bands might possibly have come from as far afield as Basingstoke and even Slough! I am, however, confident that the overwhelming majority came from within the Borough of Reading or within a ten-mile radius.

Some bands appeared under several different names. They have been treated here as different bands. Some may only ever have played one gig, others a thousand and toured the world.

And if you played on the local scene during this period and find that you haven't been mentioned, I'm very sorry. There's plenty of space to add the name of your crew in crayon, or whatever!

So, now you can have some fun trying to guess who played what: goth, psychobilly, metal, reggae, indie, folk, punk, experimental jazz, and so on. And the best of luck to you!

A

A1 Vegetables
A Fast Crowd
A G and The Astronauts
A Nation Mourns
Access
Adventure Playground
After Dark
Against the Grain
Anthill Mob
Aqua Livi
Arris
Ava Mensa

B

Back Beat Band
The Ballistics
Beat and The Devil
Beating Time
The Beevers
Between Pictures
Between the Lines
Beyond The Blue
Beyond the River
Big Noses and Funny Teeth

Bison Tribe
Bitter End
The Biz
Blind Date
Blood Oranges
Blow Up
Blues Cruise
Bore-Town Bop
Boys from Brazil

The Brothers Grimm
Brothers of Beat
Bullseye Band
Burma
Burnin' Ambition
Beating Hearts
Burnin' Tears
Butch Minds the Baby

C

The Cacophonists
Cardboard Credit Company
Carolyn Shafron
Chances Are
Chapter 1
Chapterhouse
The Chessmen

China Doll
Chocolate Teapot
Church in Ruins
Clayson and the Argonauts
The Clime
Clive Product
Clocktower

The Crooks, with Chris Broderick on bass

Coffin Nails
The Colour Mary
The Complaints
The Coolerators
Counting the Days

The Crazed
Creed of Bliss
The Crooks
Curious Oysters

D

The Dazzlers
Dealer Derek and The Decorators
Déjà vu
Diatribe
Dig Dig Dig
Dog 'ouse

Dole Queue
Double Xposure
Dumb Blondes
The Duncans

Mark Chapman on stage with Double Xposure at The Target in 1977

Firebird: James Carter, Will Barker and Andy Rowe (with drummer Steve Ricks out of shot) playing at The Target

E

80 Pop
El Seven
Elvis Has Left The Building
Emotional Jacuzzi
The Enamel Animals

Encoders
The Erection Set
The Erik Stig Band
ESP
Expresso Bongo

F

Fabulous Falling Angels
The Fabulous Mills Brothers
Fair Exchange
Fargo
Fe Scennine
Fear of Flying
Feverfew
Firebird

Flock of Rhinos
Forbidden Colours
Force Majeure
Foul Play
Four Minds Crack
Fred Kingdom
Friction Groove
Function at The Junction

G

G T Moore
Gary Jones
The Gathering
Geisha Girls
Gene Creamer and The Bunk Beds

Grizzly
General Accident
Ghosts
Go Go Amigo
The Great Mistakes

H

Hazzard
The Heart Throbs
Hollow Expressions
The Hollow Men
Home and Abroad

Hong Kong Opinion
Hook Line and Silverfish
Hot Vultures
Howlin' Horrors
Hurricane Force

A flyer promoting The Howlin' Horrors single Big Beautiful Shirt

I

In Berlin
In Hill House
Infra-Red Helicopters
Insect Matinee

Instant Fish
International Resque
Iron Heart

J

Jack Rubies
The Jackal
Jeopardy Brothers
The Jeremiahs
JFK
Jim Jiminee

Jo Jo Namoza
Johnny and The Moondogs
Johnny Cranmer Band
Joker
Joker's Wild
Justice League of America

The dynamic Jo Jo Namoza advertised to play a benefit gig
at The Paradise Club in aid of local events-listing paper Red Rag

A free DIY "K.9. badge with every *Kiss This* – cut out and wear"

K

K9s
Kaya
Killing the Rose

Kranazir
The Krewmen

L

The Larkins
Larry Miller
Lazers
Lemon Kittens
Libra
Lifecan
Linear Motion
Liquidators

Local Hero
London Street Boys
Lorelei
Lost Boys
Lost Weekend
Louis Spyro and The Midnight Express

M

Macholettes
Main Street
Midnight Sun
Mike Cooper
Moonraker

The Moonwalkers
Motley Crew
Movita
Myopic Muldoni Boys

N

Naiad
Nan Carey's Wood
Neon Reds
The Neutronz

Nightrider
Nine Steps to Ugly
Nosferatu

O

Once Every Twenty-Eight Days
One Way Street
Original Gravity

Out of Order
Overseer

P

Pandemonium Dance
    Orchestra
Parisian Living
Performing Elephants
The Pierres
Plan 9

Preacher
Predatür
Pressgang
Prime Time
The Pseudos

R

Raildogs
The Rascals
Red City Rockers
Red For Go
Reel to Real
Relay
Return of The Badmen
Ricky Rodent and The Sewer
    Rats
The Rileys
Rob Crompton
Robb Johnson

Robbed in Rome
Robert and The Remoulds
Roger Barnes
Roja Lewis' Love Earth
The Romantix
Romany
Royal Monkeys
Rubber Rubber Vortex
Rudie and The Endomorphs
Running for President
Russian Drugs

S

Samurai
The Scanners
Scatman P X
Scorpio
Scree
The Seize
Shallow Men
Shallow Tracks
Shooting The Rapids
Shrinking Men
Sideways Laughing
Signals
The Skelfs
The Soft Dogs
Some Like It Hot
Sometimes Sartre
Sonny Black's Blues Band
Special Brew
Slowdive
The Space Vultures
Spot The Dog
Spredthick
St Vitus Dance
The Stills
Straightshooter
Strypes
Sub Active
Sunfly
Surfin' Lungs
The Survivors
The Suspects
Syntax

T

Tamiko Band
Teenagers from Outer Space
Tennessee 3
Terminal 37
Terry Clarke
Thin Line
Thin Red Line
Tim Hill
Tinsel Town
Tirana
Toad
Tommy Torch and The Beacons
Too Sweet to Suck
Track 4
Traitor's Gate
Trash
Turbo
Turin
Twelfth Night

U

The Unknown
Unlikely Lads
Urban Disturbance
Urban Warrior

Tommy Torch and The Beacons

V

Valley of The Dolls

The Voice

W

Warhol's Baby
The Waltons
Warm Snorkel
West One
The Whirling Pit

White Light
White Speed
Whittaker's Patent Remedy
The Works

Z

Zeitgeist
Zerox

Zilch
Zip Code

Two Rivers Press has been publishing in and about Reading
since 1994. Founded by the artist Peter Hay (1951–2003), the press
continues to delight readers, local and further afield, with its varied list
of individually designed, thought-provoking books.